A Lifetime of Laughing and Loving with Autism

New and Revisited Stories That Will Warm and Inspire You

Compiled by R. Wayne Gilpin

A Lifetime of Laughing and Loving with Autism:
New and Revisited Stories That Will Warm and Inspire You

All marketing and publishing rights guaranteed to and reserved by:

FUTURE HORIZONSINC.

721 W. Abram Street
Arlington, Texas 76013
(800) 489-0727
(817) 277-0727
(817) 277-2270 (fax)
E-mail: *info@fhautism.com*
www.fhautism.com

© 2012 R. Wayne Gilpin
Cover and interior design, John Yacio III
Illustrations by Susie Cotton
All rights reserved.
Printed in Canada.

ISBN: 978-1935274643

Table of Contents

Introduction

The Book of Love

This book is dedicated to my son, Alex, whose life literally changed the face of the world of autism. His inspiration led to the creation of Future Horizons, which has become the largest publisher of autism materials in the world. Future Horizons now offers titles on autism, Asperger's syndrome, and sensory issues in more than 40 countries and is fortunate to include among its authors many leaders in the field.

When I originally wrote *Laughing and Loving with Autism* some 20 years ago, I ordered 500 books to be printed. I had no confidence that the public would welcome my little book of humorous and loving stories. The low print run evidenced that. However, I did have confidence that I had many friends, and I do come from a large family. So, I felt that over the years I could push copies off on people for birthdays, Christmas, graduations, and the like. Maybe a kind friend or family member would even buy a couple.

Imagine my shock when all 500 copies sold in the first 3 days! I printed another 1,000, and they vanished in about 2 weeks. Since that first printing, more than 50,000 copies of the book have brought laughter, and maybe a few misty eyes, to people all over the world.

However, the real driver behind the book and Future Horizons is my son, Alex. Although Alex has passed away now, it is his grace, kindness, sweet personality, infectious smile, and inability to see bad in others that motivates our company to this day. We believe that when the word "angel" was created, it had to be with all of the Alexes in the world in mind. Because, as wonderful as I feel my son was, his beguiling nature is shared by many who have autism. Because of those like Alex, we are gradually learning that being different is not less...and, in many ways, it can be so much more.

We should all have more of those qualities of trust, innocence, and acceptance that are shared by so many individuals who have autism. As you read this book, I hope you'll join me and others in enjoying the unique perspectives of Alex and others like him. You will see that their view of the same world we live in is often much more accurate than ours...and we can learn from them in so many ways.

Laugh, and learn. I know I did.

Wayne

Chapter 1: Logic

People with autism have their own brand of logic. It is almost always literal, and it sometimes makes more sense than ours. For those of us that are neurotypical (without autism), these stories show the logic we may miss in everyday situations.

Note: My contributions to the book that include my experiences with Alex will appear in this typeface.

After several years of working hard with my son Michael, he was finally doing fairly well fitting into the community. For his 11th birthday, I took him with me to the bakery to let him order his cake himself, with the cartoon characters he preferred. He did really well answering questions, like what cake flavor, frosting color, and filling he wanted. He pressed his face up against the glass as he surveyed the options. I could tell he was losing patience, though, when the lady working at the bakery asked him what he wanted the cake to say. He looked up at her and replied, "Are you crazy? Cakes can't talk! Just give me that one!"

Leah Devulder, California

One day, I was surprised to see that Alex came to dinner with no socks on.

"Alex, you're barefoot," I said. "You can't come to dinner like that. At least put on some socks."

"But, Dad, if I drop food, I'll get my socks dirty!"

Sometimes Alex's "logic" is difficult to counter.

I may have ruined a perfectly good learning moment by bursting out laughing during the following conversation:

Me: "Grace, honey, if I were you, I'd be more grateful than that."
Grace's sister: "Yeah, I would be grateful if I were you!"
Grace (ever literal): "No you wouldn't, because you'd be me."

Bobbi Sheahan, author of *What I Wish I'd Known about Raising a Child with Autism*, Texas

---

My son Jason asked his bald father when he was going to grow more hair on his head. His dad tried to explain that he had had hair once, but it fell out and he wouldn't be able to grow any more. For a brief second, Jason looked confused. Then he looked down at his father's arms and hands and, confident that he had figured out the loss, said, "It's okay, Dad—it fell on your arms!"

Jean Jasinski, Colorado

Doing his best unintended imitation of Jack Nicholson from the movie Five Easy Pieces, *one day Alex set a waitress back a bit by saying, "I'll have a ham and cheese sandwich—with no ham and no cheese!"*

―――――

My younger brother Jimmy has autism. I have Asperger's syndrome, so I can relate to him having special interests that are very important to him. This means I'm the one he e-mails when he wants a certain toy or object related to an interest. For instance, he currently holds a strong fascination with everything Disney. Jimmy e-mailed me with one such detailed request several years ago. He wanted a Bambi toy, but it had to be the grown-up, adult Bambi figure from the direct-to-DVD movie "Bambi II." He and my parents had had no luck at all finding one, so it was up to me. The first thing I learned is that if you go to Google search for "adult Bambi toy," you do not get links to stuff Disney sells. After a few tweaks to my search methods, I managed to find exactly one figurine of the grown-up Bambi. It was a delicate and expensive piece of china, however, and not at all suitable.

I e-mailed Jimmy to let him know that, unfortunately, there was only one grown-up Bambi figure available and it was just too expensive to get.

He e-mailed me back promptly: "I'm sorry that Bambi as a grown-up is too expensive for you to buy. Maybe you could take an extra job mowing lawns or delivering pizzas to get more money."

But that's not all. Our whole family is riddled with Asperger's and autism traits. I called my mom to tell her that Jimmy's response to my e-mail had been to advise me to take an extra job or two to make more money, to which she responded, "That's so great! He understands where money comes from!"

My husband, upon hearing about this, said, "You know, if you got a riding mower, you could mow lawns *and* deliver pizza at the same time and get paid for both."

Note: Yes, it was eventually explained to Jimmy that it is inappropriate to ask someone to take an extra job to buy him presents.

Jennifer McIlwee Myers, Aspie At Large and author of *How to Teach Life Skills to Kids with Autism and Asperger's*, California

My daughter Anne Marie plans to take care of me in my old age and has announced this to the staff at her group home, the Jay Nolan Center. She was recently very irritated with her roommate and hit her on the head with a book.

After being reprimanded, she got quiet and then remarked to a staff member, "Maybe I shouldn't take care of my mom when she's old, after all."

Margaret Pothoff, California

One day, our son Buzz showed us his own unique application of the word *autism*. I was driving with Buzz in the back seat, and we passed a bank with an electric sign out front. It was a scrolling sign that featured a thought or an ad, as many companies do. Suddenly, Buz shouted, "Look, Dad! That sign has autism!" I turned to see that it was saying, over and over, "Have a...", "Have a...", "Have a..."

Ray Grabman, Oklahoma

My son Ryan is now 12. About 3 years ago, he became fascinated with ages. (I think he knows the ages of most people in our small town.) One day he asked, "How many years ago was Daddy 16?"
I replied, "Many years ago."
"How many?"
"Many."
"Well, was that before Jesus was born?"

Kathi Kopyn, California

We were dressing up for Halloween, and I was concerned that my son didn't understand that this was an act—and not real. I don't think I got through to him. I dressed as a witch, and he was supposed to be a tiger. He was patient with the process, but his attitude toward me seemed to change as I put on the last touches of my makeup. I knew he wasn't clear on what was happening when he suddenly brightened with an idea, ran to the corner where we kept the broom, thrust it at me, and said, "Okay, now fly!"

Offered in an Autism Society of America conference workshop, author unknown

I am a speech therapist at the Sherwood Center in Kansas City. A couple of incidents always make me chuckle when I think of them.

A class of our older students with autism was copying a poem entitled "February Twilight" from the chalkboard. When asked, "What does 'twilight' mean?" one of the boys replied, "It's a zone!"

Another time, the kids in my classroom were drawing faces. "Draw some eyes," I said. So, one of my boys drew this:

Julie Thomas, Missouri

———

Alex and I were sharing some cookies. I started playing around with him, and I told him to "look at that monster over there." When he did, I took one of his cookies.

He caught on quickly, or so I thought, and was enjoying the game.

Then, to my delight, he told me to look away. When I did, with a smile, he reached up, took one of his own cookies, and hid it.

———

Travis is 13 years old, but his psychologist says that his emotional and mental age is between 5 and 7 years old. Travis has even told me before that he doesn't feel like he's 13. One day, Travis and I had this conversation:

Travis: "I am almost 13, and I think I will have another growth spurt."

Mom: "Do you feel like you're almost 13?"

Travis: "No."

Mom: "How old do you feel?"

Travis: "Six."

Mom: "Why?"

Travis: "MOOMMMM!!! I have AUTISM!!!"

Jenn Alvey, Utah

One day, my husband and I were talking about a friend of ours who was having a hard time with her United States visa papers and may have to return to her native land. Our son Matthew was very close with this friend, since she often babysat for us. When he heard that she was having trouble with immigration, Matthew "solved" the problem.

"Why don't you just pay her Visa bill so she can stay?"

Sherry and Mitch Anscher, North Carolina

Alex had two favorite meals: bacon cheeseburgers and fettuccini Alfredo. He ate reasonably well, but he did have limits on the parameters of his culinary choices. One day I asked him if he liked bananas. Obviously giving me a fast answer to shut me up, Alex quickly said, "Yes, I do." I prepared cereal with bananas for him, which he promptly pushed away with a look of something approaching disgust. "Alex, you just said that you liked bananas. What's the problem?" I asked, in my best semi-patient parent voice. Alex replied with a logic I wouldn't have dared try on my parents: "I said I like bananas, but I don't like to eat them!"

———

Jason decided this year that because his 6-year-old sister has loose teeth that will fall out, this means his balding father must have "loose hair." Sounds right.

Jean Jasinski, Colorado

———

Because Alex loved music, I took him to concerts whenever time and finances allowed. We went to rock concerts, like Nelson, Paula Abdul, and Janet Jackson. However, I also took him to hear the music of Andrew Lloyd Weber, Oklahoma, the Everly Brothers, and Wayne Newton, so he got a real variety.

However, the concert he probably enjoyed most was Janet Jackson. About 4 months after the concert, as we passed by a newsstand, I noticed a headline stating that Ms Jackson had fallen and been injured and was unable to perform. I was curious as to how Alex would respond to this unfortunate news as I pointed it out to him.

He left me standing with my mouth open as he read the headline and walked away, saying, "That's okay, Dad, we've already seen her show."

Recently, I took my son for a checkup at the doctor. During the visit, the nurse rather clinically handed my son a bottle and informed him that she needed to collect a urine sample. He looked confused but did as she asked. Later, as we were leaving, he said, "Mom, you collect vases, and I collect baseball cards. Why does that nurse collect urine? Isn't that a funny hobby?"

Lynn Spurgin, Texas

When my son David was 3½ years old, my brother, a favorite uncle, came for a visit. During the time he had been away, my brother had undergone extensive skin-cancer surgery, which resulted in some gaping wounds on the front and back of his head. For a while, he wore a bandana to avoid upsetting the children. We all watched David carefully for a reaction when his uncle finally took off the bandana.

David's already big eyes became even wider, but rather than recoiling in fear, he got closer and inspected the results of the surgery. With a voice full of innocent awe, he whispered to me, "Look, he's broken!"

What a charming and surprisingly appropriate reaction.

Author unknown

Alex has a body that any long-distance runner would die for: tall and lean and about 80% legs. Partially because of my own background running track and partially stimulated by my desire to have Alex become more physically active, I started taking him out to the track at the local school. After several outings, I decided to time him as he ran a quarter mile. His first timing set some kind of world record for slowness as he trotted around, flapping his arms, running into people, and looking everywhere except in front of him.

I then gave him a few tips on how to hold his arms, lean into the turns, stride to lessen the strain, and the like, and I told him I wanted him to try again and run as fast as he could. After some posturing, he took off and was really running well. I joined him for the last 20 yards, encouraging him as I kept an eye on the time. I reveled in his time of 1 minute 50 seconds. It was no world record, but it was a decent time for a challenged person. I congratulated Alex, who was leaning over, holding his knees, and breathing deeply.

He looked up at me with those baby-blue eyes and said, "Dad, why do I have to run so fast just to get back to where I started?"

I was showing my stepson some historical pictures in my Virginia home. Naturally, one of my favorites depicted one of Virginia's true heroes, General Robert E. Lee. I asked, "Do you know who that is?"

Without any hesitation, but with a somewhat quizzical look, he ventured, "Scrooge McDuck?"

Nat Clement, North Carolina

My 7-year-old son, Christopher, received a diagnosis of autism at age 2 and, although his language is still somewhat stilted, he often communicates well in his own way.

One day, he wanted to play with a "magic sword" that was supposed to light up—but it didn't. He brought it to me for help with a very concerned look, and said, "Batteries not included."

Linda Cavallaro, New York

My daughter Susan is very high functioning, but she still displays definite traits of autism. Recently, she said, in a very serious tone, that those with autism should be called "Autistic Americans." She went on to add, somewhat wistfully, "But they could never unite, because they can't relate."

Peggy Main, Nevada

Alex spoke with his mother after attending his first professional hockey game.

"Did you have trouble following the puck?" she asked.

(Thoughtful pause.)

"Well, Mom, I wasn't playing."

My grandson visited me in my retirement center after he'd been studying American history. We were in the library when one of my neighbors, a lovely elderly lady, approached us with a cane in her hand. "Andrew," I said, "That lady is a friend. Go over and introduce yourself."

He did very well as he marched over, put his hand out, and said, "My name is Andrew Home, what is yours?" He looked surprised as she said, "My name is Mrs Madison."

"Oh," he said, "Are you Dolly's sister?"

Bill Hale, Richmond, Virginia

Alex always amazed me with his offbeat view of life.

One day he was speaking with his sister, Jennifer, who had discovered that his roommate was very much into sports. She then asked Alex if he also liked sports. His reply was quick. "Yes, I do!"

As Alex had never shown any real interest, she was impressed and a little surprised by this response. She asked him what he liked best.

Alex replied, "Well, I do like sports, except for playing or watching. Everything else I like."

My son Sam was in a Cub Scouts group, and we were preparing him for entering the Boy Scouts. "Be Prepared" was the Boy Scout motto, and we were doing our best to live up to it. We went over all the possible questions he might be asked upon joining the Boy Scouts.

The big day came, and Sam stood in front of his den as the Scout Master asked him, "What is the Boy Scout motto?" Sam looked a little panicked and confused, so I began whispering, "Be Pr—", "Be Pr—". All of a sudden, he lit up and proudly announced, "Be Pretty!" I never saw so many people fall off their chairs laughing in my life.

Kathy Labosh, author of *The Child with Autism Learns about Faith*

As a young man with Asperger's, I saw the world in a little different light than others. This view led to an interesting exchange with a friend of my mother who, like Mom, was involved in horse breeding. Mother was actually more involved than most, and this led to a great deal of discussion about the business around the din-ner table. Being highly focused on this field caused me to misunderstand a call from my mother's friend (which led to confusion on both ends of the phone).

A friend of my mother's called excitedly one day and asked me to relay to my mother that there was a new addition to their family.

I knew Mother would want the particulars, so I asked, "What is the color?" She answered in a way that would help me decipher that it was in fact a child and not a horse, but I was having none of that.

In my confusion and my attempt to relay the right information, I asked, "Well, do you know who the father is?"

Lars Perner, Washington, DC

My youngest daughter Leesa has autism. She is 11 years old and loves to destroy her mother's closet. She does not understand the concepts of privacy or respecting other people's possessions.

To curb this behavior, my wife Karen and I tried many different strategies. We always made Leesa clean up her mess, but after picking up everything in the closet, she immediately ransacked it all over again. Timeouts were useless. We told her in our sternest voices that if she messed up Mommy's closet again, we would assign a maximum consequence as a punishment for her behavior. We applied one of these punishments each time Leesa demolished her mother's closet, but they had absolutely no effect.

When it became unbearable, we asked Leesa's teacher, Alice, how she controlled Leesa's behaviors in the classroom. Alice told us that she used simple signs to deter Leesa. For instance, Leesa loved to continuously open and close the classroom door. To curb this behavior, Alice showed us the simple picture sign of a door with the international "No" sign taped on it. This sign has been in place for more than 6 months and still works! To keep Leesa at her desk, Alice taped a simple picture sign of a desk with the words "Stay in your chair" on Leesa's desk.

I could not believe that a simple sign could stop Leesa from destroying her mother's closet. After all, speed-limit signs never stop me from speeding down the highway.

Karen and I had nothing to lose, so we taped a sign that said, "Don't mess up Mommy's closet" on the closet door. After a few weeks, I asked Karen if the sign was working. To my surprise, she said that it was.

I couldn't believe it! I started talking about this experience with my friends at work. One of them, Brad Macmillan, told me how annoyed he was with his teenage son, who took and wore his clothes. Brad told me, "My son takes practically everything I have: pants, jeans, tee shirts, shirts, socks, and even my underwear! I have to lock my bedroom door to prevent him from taking my clothes."

That evening, I went to my computer and modified the picture symbol for clothes that Leesa uses with her communication board. It is a simple picture of a pair of pants and a dress with the word "clothes" written on top. I put the international "No" sign over the pants and dress and replaced the word "clothes" with "Don't take Dad's clothes."

The next morning I gave Brad the sign, and he liked it! He put one on his closet door and one on his dresser. To Brad's surprise and mine, the sign worked immediately. Brad told me, "My son was so stunned by this sign that it took him about 10 days to come up with the courage to ask me if he could wear one of my tee shirts."

We shared our success with other staff members.

One morning shortly thereafter, I went into the bathroom at work and found a sign that said "Please wipe the sink," with a cartoon character of a maid in the lower left-hand corner. Evidently, our office secretary had gotten fed up with the puddles of water around the sink after people washed their hands.

I looked down. Sure enough, the sink and the area around it were clean, dry, and spotless! It seemed the idea for Leesa's signs had much more far-reaching effects than even I had dreamed.

Bob Carpenter

———

A mother of one of my students was in the grocery store. After finishing her shopping, she got into a line that turned out to have a customer who could not find her checkbook, identification, or anything else she needed to finish the purchase. Obviously, this caused a long wait.

To no one in particular, my student's mother said, "I always get into the wrong line."

Her daughter looked up at her with a confused look and said, "Why do you do that, Mom?"

Carol Gray, author of *New Social Stories* and *The Last Bedtime Story*, Jenison, Michigan

———

I recently overheard my 7-year-old daughter earnestly describe to her 2-year-old brother that Robin Hood and Maid Marian were in love.

"They exchanged hearts," she said.

Bobbi Sheahan, author of *What I Wish I'd Known about Raising a Child with Autism*, Texas

We worked with our son to be able to handle unusual circumstances in his life. This included an in-depth lesson on dialing 911 if there was an emergency. We spent time explaining how to call for help, information he should give, and so on.

One day not long after that, he was alone downstairs and involved in his favorite activity of watching videos. He loves his videos so much that he has them memorized and catalogued in his mind. We had a problem with renting movies, because he did not want to return them. He hid them from us. We always found them, but only after long searches. Sometimes, he even tore off the labels so we could not identify them as rented. For his purposes only, he remembered these by the barcode on the side.

On this fateful day, we heard a scream from our son, who pointed out that the video player was not functioning. I jumped up and had it running again after a few minutes. He had left the room but returned looking very relieved.

My wife passed by the phone and noticed that it was off the hook. She picked it up to find a very frustrated 911 operator, telling her not to worry because rescue personnel were on their way to handle the emergency our son had just called in.

To him, this was not just a video machine temporarily out of order. In his eyes, this was as dire an emergency as he had ever experienced, and a call to 911 was certainly called for.

Bill Davis, Pennsylvania

A father sends a small boy to bed. Five minutes later:

"Daaa-ad!"

"What?"

"I'm thirsty. Can you bring me a drink of water?"

"No. You had your chance. Lights out."

Five minutes later: "Da-aaad? I'm thirsty. Can I have a drink of water??"

"I told you NO! If you ask again, I'll have to spank you!"

Five minutes later: "Daaaa-aaaad…"

"WHAT??!!"

"When you come in to spank me, can you bring me a drink of water?"

Autism Advocacy Magazine

A little girl walked by the aquarium at the supermarket. It was loaded with lobsters, catfish, and other critters swimming around, unaware of their fate.

She stared for a little while, and then with a gentle smile, turned to her father and said, "Look, Dad, they have pets!"

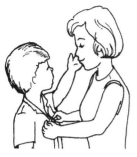

It was a very hectic morning for both my son—Alaeric—and myself, as we got ready for kindergarten. He was resistant to having his shirt buttoned and kept turning away.

With more frustration in my voice than I planned, I said, "Turn around here and face me!"

Alaeric looked momentarily surprised and confused. Then he turned around and began tenderly stroking my face.

For me, this moment defined my role in his life.

Tami McQueen, Alaska

My 8-year-old son Alex has Asperger's syndrome, and he and I went away for a weeklong visit to my brother's house. When we returned home, my husband took a look at our very tall son and said, "I could swear that you grew another foot!"

Alex looked down with a puzzled look on his face as he tried to comprehend such a ridiculous comment, and said, "No, I still have only two."

Mrs Pope, Maryland

A mother was changing the diaper of her youngest child, while her son with autism played alone in another room. The doorbell rang. Her husband called out, "Sweetheart, can you get that?"

The mother replied, "I can't—I have to change the baby."

Her son, somewhat anxiously, called out, "What's wrong with the one we have?"

Rebecca Moyes, author of *Visual Techniques for Developing Social Skills*, Pennsylvania

———

I took Alex on a vacation to Zion National Park in Utah. Unless you have been there and can draw on that memory, you can't imagine the beauty of the canyon. I really wanted Alex to share that feeling. I was constantly pointing out vistas to him, and he nodded, but I was not getting the reaction I thought the beauty deserved. Finally, we turned a corner into a truly breathtaking view, as we entered a large canyon with the cliffs changing color as they rose to the sky. I said, "Alex, look up. What do you see?" He looked up, turned to me and the other tourists who were listening, and said, boredom hanging on each word, "More rocks."

One day I was eavesdropping on two of my kids, who were enjoying a little togetherness:

"Stop arguing!"

"I'm not arguing!"

"You turn everything into an argument."

"No, I don't. Not everything."

Bobbi Sheahan, author of *What I Wish I'd Known about Raising a Child with Autism*, Texas

The Wisdom of Temple

Anyone who has attended a Future Horizons conference knows that Dr Temple Grandin is one of our favorite people. She is special not only for her caring for people with autism and Asperger's syndrome, but also for the unique perspective that she brings to the world. At one of our recent conferences, an attendee very gently asked Temple if she feels she missed out by not going to the senior prom, college parties, and the like, which are so much a part of many young people's lives.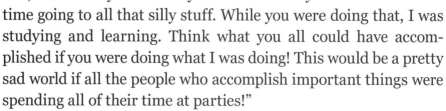

Temple seemed bemused by the question and replied with perfect Temple logic, "No, I don't. In fact, I feel sorry for all of you who wasted your time going to all that silly stuff. While you were doing that, I was studying and learning. Think what you all could have accomplished if you were doing what I was doing! This would be a pretty sad world if all the people who accomplish important things were spending all of their time at parties!"

Alex's mother offers the following wonderful stories...

Alex and I were watching a TV special on Frank Sinatra, 3 weeks after the crooner's death. I was curious about how he would like this style of music from the late and great entertainer.

"Alex, I bet seeing old film clips of this man make you think he is a real old-fashioned guy."

"It sure does. I also think he is a real old-fashioned dead guy."

=

Alex could sometimes be a challenge to one's ego. I had called and left him a message on his answering machine, but he had not replied.

When I finally reached him I was slightly bothered, and I asked why he had not called.

His answer stunned me. "Oh, was that you? I thought the voice sounded familiar..."

=

Alex was preparing for a trip to California, obviously with some apprehension he had not mentioned before. I held up an invitation he had received recently, and I said, "Alex, this invitation is for a nice TEACCH dinner when you get back from your trip. It's something to look forward to."

Very calmly, he answered, "Well, that is if I don't get killed in an earthquake."

Hoping to help Alex with his Christmas shopping, I suggested that he buy a Neil Diamond recording for my husband and me. He answered, "Ah, Mom, I'd really rather spend my money on myself."

———

Alex often showed a surprising depth of understanding, in spite of his challenges. He loved to create puns. Once, I was talking to him about his passion to do things on time and very exactly. He gave me that grin and said, "Mother, that is because I have precise-ism!"

———

I told Alex that we had an appointment with the Social Security Administration. He asked what it was for. I told him it was to get government benefits for him. He didn't know what that meant. After a long pause, he asked, "You're not going to put me in the army, are you?"

Starla Clement, North Carolina

A Different View of "Truth"

Children with autism will rarely lie, or, if they do, they do it very poorly and are delightfully confused when the "shallow" untruth is not accepted. Here are several stories that speak to this.

When my son, Chris Purdue, was 16 years old, he attended a moderately handicapped program based in a large high school. This particular class was on the first floor of the school, and, since it dealt with abstract concepts about money, he was rather bored. Also, Chris always loves to be up high, wherever he goes. One day, instead of going into his own classroom, he decided to attend another class on the second floor "to see if it was more interesting."

When the teacher came into the classroom and saw Chris, she asked him, "Well, who are you?" Chris, who has good language abilities and appears to function normally, sat up proudly and said, "My name is Craig Alexander." (Chris knew another boy named Craig—as for where he got Alexander, who knows?)

Looking a little surprised, the teacher said, "Craig, I don't think you belong here—you must be in the wrong room." Chris replied with assurance, "No, I'm in the right room—I've been here before." The teacher said, "No, I don't think so—if you'd been here before, I'd have seen you." Chris then said, "No, you're wrong. I've been here before. You've just not seen me because sometimes I'm invisible."

The teacher was very confused, the class loved it, and Chris could never comprehend how the teacher knew he didn't belong in that class.

Bev Purdue, Indiana

Alex was "stimming"—rocking back and forth waving his arms—as I was telling him the story of Pinocchio and how his nose grew when he lied.

"Alex," I said, "You can stop stimming."

"Dad, I'm not doing anything."

"You were stimming."

"Was not."

Then, a thought spread across his face, and, with a look of fear, Alex slowly raised his finger up to feel his nose.

———

My adult son with autism works at the Eton Center and is generally good about going to his job. However, one day he was reluctant about going, so I asked his supervisor to talk to him. This was their conversation, after I handed my son the phone:

"Why aren't you coming in?"

"Can't, my mother's been robbed and raped by burglars."

"I just spoke to your mother."

"No, I'm telling the truth, she's lying at my feet, dead!"

"Can I speak to your mother?"

"No, she's calling the fireman because our house is on fire and it's burning down."

After some conversation, his supervisor made it clear that he wasn't going to buy into these stories.

"What is the real reason you can't come into work?"

"I just don't want to."

"Well, how would you like to come on in and we'll have lunch and talk about this?"

"Oh, that sounds nice. I'll be there."

Sandra Davidson, New Jersey

Chapter 2: Music

All children with autism—almost without exception—love music. The following stories highlight that love.

Alex loves singing and was in his 6th-grade chorus. It came time for the Christmas recital. The group practiced for weeks, and Alex, who has an incredible memory for songs, knew every song perfectly. To add to the excitement, the recital was to be held in the town square of Chapel Hill, North Carolina, in front of a large crowd. Finally the big night came, and Alex assumed his place in the group.

The recital began, and the chorus proceeded to sing its repertoire. However, amazingly, Alex didn't open his mouth to sing— he simply stood there with a big smile on his face. His mother, Starla, was a little taken aback and anxious to identify the problem. After the recital, she worked her way through the crowd to Alex's side. Before she could say a word, Alex said, "Wasn't it good, Mom? Did you like it?"

Her confusion only increased. Starla said, "But Alex, you didn't sing a word."

Alex looked up with surprise and said, "I might not have looked like I was singing, but I was...I was singing inside."

After a moment of reflection, she smiled, gave him a big hug, and took her silent singer home.

I'm a mother of a 3½-year-old who received a diagnosis of pervasive developmental delay and autism. He doesn't speak 80% of the time. But, Rusty does offer some nonmeaningful speech. If he's in a particularly good mood, he will sit with a smile on his face, flap his hands, and say "Diga diga diga" over and over again.

One day, we went out for an afternoon drive. As usual, we were listening to music. Rusty sat in his booster seat, the warm Hawaii breeze blowing in his face. He began to "flap" and repeat "Diga, diga, diga." About that time, an advertisement came over the radio for the Whitney Houston movie, "The Bodyguard."

We then heard a part of her new song, where she sings, "I will always love you," and the "you" part is high-pitched and stretched out. Rusty continued flapping but suddenly changed his "song" to "Diga, diga, diga...you!!"

The "you" Rusty sang was a perfectly pitched Whitney Houston imitation, the high note held for exactly the right length. My husband and I rolled with laughter. This lovely memory has stayed with our family ever since.

Carla Clancy, Hawaii

———

When Alex was in the 2nd grade, he loved music of all kinds, but mostly rock. His favorite singer was George Michael. As it was the beginning of the Christmas season, his teacher polled the students on their favorite songs. The first student said, "Rudolph the Red Nosed Reindeer." The second said, "Away in the Manger." The third brightly said, "Good King Wenceslas." Then the teacher asked, "Alex, can you tell us your favorite song?" He looked up at her with his bright blue eyes and completely innocent face and said, "I Want Your Sex" (George Michael's big 1987 hit).

The teacher could barely contain herself. The aide had to leave the room, she was laughing so hard.

———

My husband is in the vocal group "The Spinners." Our son, Purvis, has autism, and he is virtually nonverbal—except when he hears The Spinners' songs. He joins in singing every word, the language clear and perfectly in beat.

Claudreen Jackson, Michigan

———

I work with a 34-year-old man who loves music—especially the songs of Andy Williams, Glen Campbell, and Johnny Mathis. In fact, in the morning he has breakfast with them. Sort of. He lines up their albums around the breakfast table and tells them about his upcoming day.

A new staff member asked him if he had ever met Andy Williams. He responded that he had seen him in concert and had actually met him. The staffer was impressed and asked him how he felt, meeting such a big star. However, the staffer was immediately corrected as he was told that Andy Williams was not a big star at all.

All within hearing range were shocked to hear this statement by such a big fan, until he clarified, "He is not big at all. He is just a little, short guy—much smaller than I am."

Debbie Wilson, Illinois

Chapter 3: Family

When you live with a person with autism in your family, you have different challenges and joys than "normal" families. One thing is certain: You will probably not get too many big egos in the family.

I was running happily on my new treadmill. Decked out in trendy workout clothes, I felt a sense of pride and accomplishment as I turned up the speed to make the belt move faster and faster.

My daughter brought me back to earth as she came into the room and voiced her literal interpretation of my efforts.

"My mother—the gerbil."

Diana Daggett, New Mexico

Alex has an Uncle Gary, who enjoys him very much and likes teasing him—as he does all his other nieces and nephews. Alex loves the attention. As the family jokester, Gary usually one-ups the other clan members but, intentionally or not, Alex got him with this interchange.

"Alex, you sure are good-looking, with your pretty blonde hair and big blue eyes. I sure wish I was as good-looking as you are."

Alex's reply came with a perfectly straight face: "I'm sorry, Uncle Gary, but you're not."

My son Ryan was invited by his grandmother to come to her house to spend the night. This was during a period when he really didn't like being away from me, and he was resistant. My mother offered this logic: "Now, Ryan, my house couldn't be the worst place you could go, could it now, dear?"

Ryan pondered the question for a long minute and then very solemnly said, "No, hell would be worse."

Lisa Starnes, Texas

Alex tries to be considerate of others' feelings, although he shows it in humorous ways sometimes. His efforts in this area led to this conversation, after a few friends from his junior-high school took him to a movie.

"Alex, how did you like the show?"

"It was good, Dad."

"Who did you enjoy going to the movies with the most?"

"Dad, I always like being with you best!"

"Well, Alex, that's nice. Thank you." (I felt like a great dad.)

"Dad, I only said that because I didn't want to hurt your feelings."

Alex giveth, and Alex taketh away.

———

My nephew and I were singing together at a family gathering. My energetic but not sophisticated voice rang out next to his head. I was impressed with his singing, and after we finished our song, I told him so. "Alex, I wish I could sing as well as you do."

With a sigh, he responded, "I sure wish you could sing as well as me, too."

Marjorie Langhorne, California

———

Alex had an interesting perception of family relationships. I asked him how he might like to be an uncle one day. He said that would be okay. His answer felt to me like he might not understand the relationship, so I asked him if he knew how someone became an uncle. He looked puzzled for a moment and then brightened up as he said, "Grow a moustache?"

(This seemed like a logical conclusion to Alex, as most of his uncles sported moustaches at the time.)

When my son was about 7 or 8, we were working very hard on teaching the value of taking turns. He tended to plunge ahead, without thinking of another child's need to take a turn at whatever game they were playing. Finally, we thought we had gotten the message across to him.

Some time later, we were at a large gathering for Thanksgiving. Since it was only family, we relaxed and let our son play in the back bedroom with his cousins while we got the rare opportunity to visit with other adults.

Suddenly, we heard the terrifying sound of a child struggling to breathe. Rushing into the room, we arrived just in time to hear our son, who had his arm around his somewhat red-faced cousin's neck, say proudly, "Okay, I'm done choking you. Mother says it's good to take turns. So now it's your turn to choke me!"

Obviously, another lesson in taking turns was necessary.

Teresa Loftus, Washington

I have this habit, which is disconcerting to others, of turning my blinker on before I actually have to. This is not an age thing, as I have done it since I was a teenager. My daughter Jennifer hates it and brings it up whenever she can.

We were driving in California and I, by mistake, not only hit the turn signal before a turn, but it actually wound up being just a bend in the road, and not a turn after all. We all laughed, and Jennifer said, "He did that because he's my dad!"

Alex, from the back seat, calmly said, "No, Jennifer, he did that because he's dumb."

On my mother's birthday, I sat with my siblings with a big smile on my face...but no present.

I waited as all the others gave their presents, and after my mother had opened them, she turned to me very patiently and in a kind voice said, "Wendy, do you have something for your mother?"

I replied, "Yes, Mother—I am thinking of giving you something very nice!"

Before my now puzzled mother could respond, I added, "Last year when I gave you a present, you said it was the thought that counts—and I am thinking of a great present for you! You would have really loved it!"

Wendy Lawson, contributor to *Different...Not Less*, Victoria, Australia

---

Alex, his sister Jennifer, my friend Polly, and I went out to dinner. It was an excellent restaurant, in one of the nicest parts of San Diego. As it was a fairly upscale French restaurant, we worried that Alex would not find a selection that he would enjoy.

However, our fears were put to rest as he spied linguini on the menu. He talked about it constantly before and after we ordered, but when it arrived, he stopped and gave the linguini his absolute attention.

After eating, I went to the restroom. Alex was so absorbed, he didn't even see me leave. However, he looked up to find me gone. He turned to his sister and asked where I was.

Jennifer told him and he responded, "That's good, I sure would hate to lose my dad. I love him very much."

This was a fairly rare expression from Alex, and both Jennifer and Polly were really touched by the depth of his words.

To which he added, "I love Dad almost as much as...as much as...THIS LINGUINI!"

A number of years ago, my daughter Jennifer was required to write a paper for her English class. She chose Alex as her subject. Until recently, I didn't know the paper existed. It only came to the surface as I was doing research for this book. It serves as a very appropriate addition to Laughing and Loving with Autism. *I'm sure you'll enjoy it...almost as much as I did.*

Today, I spoke with the only real Steppenwolf I know—only I had forgotten that I knew him. This person is my little brother, Alex. People think there is something very wrong with him because he can't (or won't) relate to other people. I see a lot of him in me and am always surprised and a bit pleased whenever I become aware of these similarities. This is because I like to view my brother as being blessed rather than cursed. Alex was born with autism.

In case you are sitting there scratching your head and wondering why that word sounds familiar, I will refresh your memory. Autism is the disorder Dustin Hoffman had in "Rain Man." However, by no means did I grow up with a young Raymond Babbitt. Alex can't do anything wonderful with numbers, and he does not read phone books or count toothpicks. Yet, he is cut off from most of the world.

That is about all I can say for certain. I do not know whether he was born away from us on the Mountain or if he has not even seen the fire that we think is light. I do not know this because he won't tell me. He does not write pages and pages filled with wise words. He does not paint emotional pictures. He does not compose music or make clay sculptures. I suppose he feels no need to express his emotions. He only feels them.

You can read me anything that any scholar of autism has said to the contrary, but I am sure that Alex feels. He gets carried away by his emotion and forgets everything our parents have tried to teach him about how one should act in society. How can he restrain himself according to society's rules if he isn't even aware of their presence?

He often skips absurdly around the house, stopping every once in a while to jump up and down in one spot while fixating on the ceiling. Usually while he is doing this, he is laughing. I don't know what he is laughing at. I guess it's just another of these things he sees that we don't. I wish he would tell me what he is thinking—what he finds funny. But, he often stays in his small upstairs room, and I don't even know if he has any desire to come out.

I said in the beginning of this paper that I saw much of Alex in me. I have always wondered if that also made me somehow different from the rest of the world. I usually don't like people to bother me. As a child, I always upset my mother by closing myself in my room for hours on end. I never like to hear any noise from the outside world when I am trying to be alone. I was (and still am) forever shutting the door to my room, trying to close off the rest of the family, the TV, and any music that is playing in the house. I never understood why this upset my family. Alex was the first person to ever shut the door on me. He was the first person who ever told me to go away because he wanted to be alone. Though no one else understood that, I did.

Alex and I are also both very sensitive to sound. Any loud noise, even noises that don't bother others, will frighten us both. One recent example of this is when my father took us to see a movie at a theater that both Alex and Dad had been to—but I hadn't. For the 10 minutes before the movie started, Alex sat hunched over in his seat with his hands over his ears. Dad told me that he was afraid of a buzzing sound that went off at that theater before the movie started. I knew that any sound that frightened him would probably also scare me, but as I look a lot like an adult type of person, I knew that I could not hunch over in my seat with my hands over my ears. Being the fool I am, I leaned over and teased my brother for being silly. I made myself forget about it, and about 2 minutes later, a loud buzzer went off. As my father loves to tell it, I yelped and jumped about a foot off my seat.

This sensitivity to noise also has its good sides. My brother and I love music and will sit and listen to it for hours. I know he gets something out of the music he listens to because he always stops what he is doing and pays very close attention. His music is very important, and he must listen undisturbed. Sometimes I forget this and start singing. Of course, Alex is always there to kindly remind me to shut up.

Many times, people (yes, even me) have asked my brother questions in an attempt to coax a piece of him out into the open for us to see. His answers are so trite and bizarre that I wonder if they reflect what he really thinks or if he is making fun of the rest of us. Once, when my father and Alex were driving through a piece of beautiful country, with hills, trees, and lakes, Dad asked Alex to turn to his right and describe what he saw. My brother looked in that direction, turned back to my father, and answered, "A window."

When explaining why I decided to change my story line for this paper, I indicated that I had recently spoken with Alex and realized that I must write about him. However, I did not speak with my brother over the phone, and since he does not live in this state (Texas, I mean—I'm not being philosophical, necessarily), I could not have spoken to him in person. Rather, I saw and conversed with Alex in a rather bizarre place—in a strange and vivid dream.

In this dream, I found myself walking down the empty streets of my hometown of Baltimore. I seemed to be wandering, but I felt a sense of going somewhere. I turned a corner and saw a restaurant that had light coming from the window. It was bright, harsh light, but it was light nonetheless, so I decided to investigate.

The inside was almost as eerie as the streets outside. Everything was perfectly clean and orderly, and the few people inside were silent. Normally, I would have passed by and kept to myself, but something about the place intrigued me. It seemed like the kind of place where anything was possible.

I ordered a cup of coffee and drifted into my own world as someone set the machine to make my hot bitter drink. Suddenly, I was startled as one of the patrons came and sat down beside me. For some reason, this seemed like the wrong place for conferring with others. In other restaurants it would have been strange, but somehow here it seemed unacceptable...and I liked it that way.

However, the man coming up to speak with me was not at all threatening, and his natural smile was comfortable and warm. He started to speak, and his voice was familiar—but the words were not.

His face looked like I should know it somehow, but it was too... old? He kept on talking, and for some reason I thought he should not be using words so well, and he should not be speaking in such long, beautifully formed, eloquent sentences. Then, I felt a tremendous sense of joy as I realized who was sitting next to me and who was saying such wonderful things.

But, it couldn't be.

"Alex?"

He stopped talking. "Yes?"

In the back of the restaurant, I heard the beeping of the coffee machine.

Why didn't someone turn it off?

Beep. Beep. Beep. Beep.

"This is wonderful, Alex. How did it happen? You can converse with me. You are finally part of our world!" For some reason there was urgency to my speech, as if I had little time left.

His last words came to me as I realized the beeping was my alarm clock, and I was dreaming and had to get up.

"No, Jennifer, you have entered into my world."

Chapter 4: Religion

In our society, there are few areas where propriety is more strictly observed than in church and/or with religion. Therefore, it is naturally the perfect place to have humor hit its mark.

When our son Chris was about 6, he developed an interest in televised football games. He watched the games while standing in front of the TV and seemed to be very interested in all of the running, jumping, and falling. The slow-motion replays especially held his attention. He flapped his  arms like kids with autism do, rocked back and forth on his feet, and uttered remarks like, "Gee whiz!", "Oh God!", "How could he drop that?", and "Fall down!" At times, he almost sounded like a Steelers fan.

Quite frequently, after a play, Chris would shout, "Touchdown!", imitating my victory chant whenever the Steelers scored. Most of the time, of course, a touchdown had not been made, and I would say, "No Chris. That's no touchdown." He often gave me a perplexed look, and I never got the impression that he understood the difference between a touchdown or a first down or even a commercial. That is, not until one Sunday morning in church.

We got the bright idea that Chris might be more interested in religion if we sat in the front pew. At least we wouldn't have to worry about him stealing purses and wigs from the ladies sitting in front of us. It actually worked for a few weeks. Chris seemed to enjoy all the goings-on at the altar. He was especially interested in the organist and the choir.

Chris had been watching the Mass unfold very attentively. His eyes followed the priest as he walked over to our side of the church and stopped in front of us, raising both arms over his head to give us a blessing. Seeing this "signal," Chris jumped up and, in his loudest voice and clearest diction, shouted, "TOUCH-DOWN!" The priest, with his arms still upraised, gave a startled look our way. I looked down at Chris reproachfully. He looked up at me and then "corrected" the situation as he shouted out, "That's no touchdown!"

Benoit Beaudoin, Pennsylvania

When our son, Mitch, became a young man, he moved into his current group home. They habitually said "grace" each night, and each person was asked to thank God for the food before eating. One evening, it was Mitch's turn. When he didn't say anything, one of the staff prompted, "Mitch, who do we thank for our food tonight?" Mitch answered, "I thank Bill." Everyone was a little confused until they remembered that "Bill" was the cook. Great logic.

Phyllis-Terri Gold, PhD, New York

My son Brian enjoys going to church at least partially because of his love of music. So I take him to our Catholic service whenever possible. Normally, I take him in the side door after the service starts, and we quietly find seats in the back. However, one Sunday we walked in with everyone else because we were attending with our out-of-town guests.

Everything seemed to be going well as we proceeded into the narthex and greeted the other parishioners.

Everyone in front of us was quiet and respectful as they made the sign of the cross with the holy water. All was fine until Brian spotted the water. He loves swimming, and taking baths takes a strong second.

Before I could reach him, Brian's eyes lit up. He plunged his face into the holy water and vigorously began blowing bubbles. Other than the sounds he made, you could have heard a pin drop as everyone in the narthex froze. Then, just as quickly as he went in, he popped his head out with a huge grin. He looked up at me, said, "Good," and proceeded to take a seat in the last row.

Somehow, I didn't think God or the Catholic church would mind.

Mira Blaine, Alberta, Canada

Ruth Sullivan is one of the founders of the Autism Society of America. She and her son Joe have been on "Oprah" and other talk shows. Joe was one of the models Dustin Hoffman used in preparing for his role in "Rain Man." This story involves one of her trips to church with Joe.

We attended a confirmation service at church. Afterward, the priest left the altar and went slowly down the aisle to pleasantly but solemnly greet the parishioners as they left. As we were in the front of the church, we were among the last to leave, but there was still a crowd around the priest as we got to the door. Without warning, Joe, with a smile, reached through the crowd to touch the priest and said in a loud voice, "French toast." Our otherwise verbal clergyman wasn't sure how to answer this unusual statement.

I, on the other hand, was aware that French toast was one of Joe's favorite things—so I knew that, in his own way, he was trying to say that he enjoyed the service.

Ruth Sullivan, West Virginia

Our son's name is Mitch. When he was very little, I used to pray aloud by his bedside each night. He gave me no indication that he even heard what I said, which always began, "Dear God, please help Mitch in all the ways that you can and help us, too," and so on. This continued for about 2 years, until one evening, when I sat down on the edge of his bed as usual. Mitch startled me by telling me emphatically, "No Dear God tonight!" and promptly turned over to go to sleep.

Phyllis-Terri Gold, PhD, New York

Church became a true "experience" with our 6-year-old daughter Christina. We would bet beforehand how much of the Mass we would be able to get through before our little angel decided she had had enough holiness for the day. Most of the time, we made it about halfway through the service before we had to leave.

However, one Sunday was different—or so we thought. Christina was quiet and pensive. We actually got to stay for the entirety of the sermon, which was unusual. At the end, the priest solemnly said, "Let us pray for our intentions," and the Father and the congregation became quiet as they prayed. The lengthening silence was more than Christina could stand. Suddenly, her voice pealed out over the congregation in a perfect imitation of the character "Sergeant Carter" from the TV show "Gomer Pyle":

"I CAN'T HEARRRR YOUUU!"

Sometimes, we think Christina is only visiting us for our amusement, education, and growth.

Tom and Julie D'Amura, Oklahoma

I run a camp for young adults. One of them, whom we will call Bob, had a problem with ordering things in the food line or anywhere else where he had to ask for service. So we practiced with Bob, and he seemed to be getting better. However, I didn't know how much better until I, at his mother's request, took him to a Catholic Mass that was being conducted close to the camp.

Bob decided to take communion, and I thought it best to walk to the front of the church with him, although I am not Catholic. We were waiting at the altar as the priest approached with the wafer. Before he could offer it, Bob said, in a voice you could hear in the back of the church, "I'll have one body of Christ, please!"

Dr James Ball, New Jersey

An exasperated mother, whose son was always getting into mischief, finally asked him, "How do you expect to get into Heaven?"

The boy thought it over and said, "Well, I'll just run in and out and in and out and keep slamming the door until St Peter says, 'For Heaven's sake, Jimmy, come in or stay out!'"

Autism Advocacy Magazine

Mom (after buying her son Travis new gloves): "Travis, are those gloves working okay for you?"

Travis (smiling and giggling): "Mom, they're not mechanical!"

Jenn Alvey, Utah

Our son James was going to have his tonsils removed. Our new minister kindly and dutifully came to the hospital to give his support. After some opening words of encouragement to James, we had a general conversation that covered several subjects. Somehow, the subject of drinking and driving came up, along with the dangers associated with children. We were all discussing this important matter very seriously, when James suddenly interrupted, "But Dad, you drink and drive all the time!"

In shock, I looked from James to the minister. He looked as surprised as I did, and I noticed that he was no longer looking my way. Abashedly, I asked James when he had seen me drink and drive. In his typically honest way, he said, "Just this morning, you drank a Pepsi as we drove to the hospital!"

I was relieved to see the smile on the minister's face as he realized that in James's literal world, "drinking was drinking."

John Guyest, Pennsylvania

———

Our rector wanted to make a point to the children assembled around him during the Sunday morning service, so he used a parable. To make it dramatic, he told of a little bird that got caught in a snowstorm.

My heart stopped as my son Ben raised his hand. Every eye in the church turned to my son as he said, "I'm sorry, Father, but birds would not be out in a snowstorm. They fly south for the winter."

The congregation roared with laughter as the somewhat red-faced Father Henry sheepishly conceded, "You're right, Ben." Needless to say, this somewhat detracted from the drama of his story.

Laura Schroeder, Texas

At a church service for handicapped people, a mother and her son Neil were sitting in front of a handicapped child who made a distressing high-pitched bleating sound every time there was a lull in the proceedings. This conversation ensued.

Neil: "Mother, there's a lamb in the church."

Mother: "Huh?"

Neil: "I didn't know they allowed sheep in the church."

Mother: "Shhh!"

Neil: "Maybe it is the lamb of God..."

Helen Benson, Upson, England

Getting up early was never easy for Alex. One morning, I remarked that he looked like a zombie.

"What's a zombie?" he asked.

I tried to put my response in a way that someone who had never seen a horror movie might understand. "Alex, it is when a person dies and is buried, but rises from the grave to walk among the living with their hands held out like this," I said as I held my arms out.

Incredulously he asked, "So, Jesus was a zombie?"

Chapter 5: School

Turning our children loose in an educational atmosphere offers untold opportunities for laughter. The school structure is usually fine with kids who have autism, as long as it meets the guidelines of what these children, in their unique way, consider to be sensible. When it doesn't meet that standard, look out! You'll all enjoy these, but if you're a teacher or educational professional, you're really going to love what follows.

My son's father, Mark, is a 7th-grade regular-education teacher in Sioux City, Iowa. Our son, Ryan, is in his class. This situation can be awkward for any parent and child, but with Ryan's willingness to say whatever pops into his mind, it can be outright "dangerous" for Mark. For instance, Mark put on a few extra pounds over this past winter, and Ryan likes to tease his father about it.

Recently, Mark was conducting class and asked, "Guess what I saw the other day for the first time in a long time?"

Ryan replied, "Your feet?"

Mark and Barbara Renfro, Iowa

I was helping Alex with his homework, when we got to math. The drill required learning math terms, with the first being "hypothesis." Since Alex has a problem with things that are not concrete, I thought this was beyond him, but I tried anyway. "Alex, it's an idea that could happen." I explained it as basically as I could. He regarded me with a blank stare.

Later, to my chagrin, there was a recap exercise. The first question was, "Make up your own hypothesis." I turned to Alex without much hope. "Alex, you have to give me a hypothesis."

He replied, "Maybe I will."

———

When Travis was in 2nd grade, his teacher wanted the class to finish the sentences from various sayings. Here are some of the ones Travis wrote. It makes me smile when he sometimes takes things very literally. His answers are in quotes...

* Don't throw the baby out with the..."binkie!"
* He who marries for money..."will marry a rich woman!"
* If you can't stand the heat..."you will sweat!"
* Silence is..."quiet!"
* Money is the root of all..."famous people!"
* When the cat's away..."it's running away!"
* Early to bed and early to rise makes..."the sun!"
* Laugh and the world laughs with you. Cry and you..."puke!" (Note: Travis used to throw up whenever he cried hard.)
* Every cloud has a..."thing of water!"
* A door never closes without..."shutting it!"
* You've made your bed, now..."your mom is happy!"
* When it rains it..."is pouring water!"

* A penny saved is…"1 cent!"
* With age comes…"older!"
* No news is…"terrible!"
* Good things come to those who…"are nice!"
* The grass is always greener on…"the ground!"
* A fool and his money are…"stealing!"

Jenn Alvey, Utah

Recently, my 7-year-old son, Tim, had his first accident on the playground at school. He fell from some bleachers and acquired a few scrapes. In my attempts to find out how high he had been climbing, I asked him, "How far did you fall?"

Tim gave me that tolerant look he uses for silly questions and replied, "All the way, Mom."

Nora Rege, Oregon

Often, having a child with autism causes an otherwise normally functioning parent to respond to a situation in abnormal ways. Peg says this story is about her son. I'm not so sure.

This story is about my son, Bobby, who is attending a 4-year-old pre-primary–school class for kids with all kinds of disabilities. Every day, the teacher sends home a note that explains his behavior during class. One day, his teacher, Mrs Munson, sent home a note to indicate that "Bobby was spitting on friends today."

I read the note, but unlike the average parent who may have been upset or angry, I was delighted. I started to hug Bobby as I jumped up and down, yelling, "Bobby, you have friends. You have friends!"

Peg and Tim Jindra, Michigan

This story involves my son, Scot, who is now 19 years old. He has always has been very verbal, but he exhibits many behaviors of autism.

At the time this happened, Scot was 8 or 9 years old and was attending a special-education class for students with autism. One of Scot's friends in that class was a cute little Asian boy named Michael. Since Scot had a fixation with school buses, this was his favorite topic of conversation, especially at the dinner table.

One evening, during such a conversation at dinner, his bus story centered around Michael. At one point in the story, Scot said, "Michael rides a handicapped bus." To encourage the conversation and to see what his response would be, I asked, "Is Michael handicapped?"

He looked at me with a look of total disbelief and replied emphatically, "NO, HE'S CHINESE!"

Betty Manning, Virginia

I was informed by Alex's special-education teacher that Alex was supposed to receive an award at the 7th-grade awards ceremony. It was with a mixture of pride and apprehension that I took my seat. How would he act, going up on the stage? What would this mean to him? My concern increased as I realized that his seat was all the way in the back of the auditorium, requiring a long trip down three aisles to get to the stage.

The proceedings unfolded, with the kids receiving awards in everything from academics and sports to school service. Being 7th graders, they all accepted their awards while looking at their feet, the ceiling, or their best friend, saying very little or nothing at all and leaving the stage.

Finally, it was Alex's turn. The teacher began, "This next award is for a very special young man. When I was told I was going to have a student with autism, I didn't know what to expect. Alex has been a joy. He's very mannerly and sweet and tries his very best. This award is for Alex Gilpin for effort, manners, and attitude."

I turned to see the biggest smile I've ever seen coming down the aisle. His loping walk was far quicker than usual, and he negotiated the path to the stage perfectly. He shook his teacher's hand and turned to leave. However, he stopped dead in his tracks. My heart stopped along with his stride. What was wrong? Then he turned and did something no other student had managed. In a voice loud enough to be heard in the back of the auditorium, he said, "Thank you. Thank you very much!"

There must have been an air pollution problem in that auditorium, because my eyes were very misty.

As I was teaching my son about letters, I tried to instruct him to listen to the first letter of a word, as this would help him to sound it out. I felt like I was getting nowhere fast. Finally, I thought I hit on the perfect idea. My son's name is Warren Werner, so I said, "Listen—your name is Warren Werner. What is the first letter of each?"

He brightened up as he gave the literal and correct answer to my question: "E."

Lee Werner, Illinois

My favorite stories are the ones that show how my son, Ted, understands more, much more, than he's given credit for. In fact, I rejoice every time he outsmarts me. This happens more often than one might expect, and often unpredictably.

Recently, Ted and I had a discussion about his younger brother, who is a student at the University of Washington. I explained that he was taking science classes. Receiving a blank look, I assumed a lack of understanding and asked, "Ted, do you know what 'science' means?"

"No", he answered. Groping to define the word, I began, "Well, 'science' means 'study' or 'knowledge.' So, a scientist is a person who knows a lot about a certain area. For example, there are scientists who study different forms of life. They are called 'biologists.'"

His eyes still looked blank, with no apparent glimmer of recognition and very little interest. I tried an example that might mean more to Ted. "There's a name for all scientists. For an example, there's a name for people who study animals. They are called 'zoologists.'"

Still trying to communicate my wisdom to my son with the sphinx-like smile, I added, "There's even a word for people who study reptiles." I tried to think of the term, couldn't, and looked for another example. "There's a special name for scientists who study fish, too." Again, I, the teacher, couldn't come up with it.

Ted noticed my thoughtful pause. As I tried to remember the difficult word, he leaned forward and said, "Do you mean an *ichthyologist?*"

And with that, I received another lesson in underestimating Ted.

Charley Hart, Washington

On the way home from school one day, my three boys, including my son Jeremy, who has autism, were discussing what they had learned. My oldest said, "Just say no to drugs."

The youngest piped up with another important rule, "Never get into a car with a stranger."

I asked Jeremy if he knew of any important rules. He responded, "Never call a girl stupid."

I found out later from Jeremy's teacher that he had gotten into a lot of hot water that day as he learned this particular rule.

Bonita Gallen, Texas

We try to mainstream our son into society at every opportunity. This desire led us to have Ted attend Sunday school. It didn't seem to be going too well. When we asked him simple questions about the lesson, he gave no responses. So, I decided to sit in on the class with him and ask him questions immediately afterward.

That Sunday, the lesson included a film about Abraham and Isaac. As the plot unfolded, Abraham took his beloved son up to the mountain to be sacrificed, as commanded by God. I began to worry. I thought, "What have I done to this child, forcing him to watch something he's bound to misunderstand?"

It got worse. After Isaac got a reprieve, Abraham slaughtered a ram that was caught in a bush by his horns. Then Sarah's jealousy of a slave woman and her son caused her to insist that Abraham banish them both to the desert forever. Mercifully, the movie stopped, and I turned to Ted reluctantly and asked, "What was the movie about?"

Ted turned his head and uttered, "Cannibals."

With all apologies to theologians, if one had to reduce that complicated storyline to one succinct term, we believe "cannibals" would be hard to beat.

Charley Hart, Washington

My daughter is pretty good at getting ready for school. I lay out her clothes, and she follows my directions. Recently, she decided to pick out her clothes and get ready herself—even better. This usually required some prompting from me. However, this newfound independence led to an interesting problem.

About 3 weeks after she'd start-ed dressing herself, she came home from school appearing very unhap-py. I inquired as to why she had a long face. She almost cried as she related how she wore a dress every day, while the other kids got to wear pants and shorts. I was shocked.

"Darling, you have all kinds of other clothes. Why don't you wear those?" I asked. She looked as shocked at my statement as I had at hers. "Mother, it's your fault," she asserted. "Every morning you tell me to go get dressed!"

Virginia Unverzagt, Illinois

Alex has grown into a very social young man, although his friendliness often takes an open, charming, and—according to "normal" standards—inappropriate manner. He'll talk to anyone in a relaxed way, without embarrassment.

A new teacher started at his junior-high school, and, between classes, she assumed her place in the hall to observe student traf-fic. She was surprised to have this tall young man come up to her, put out his hand, and say, "Hello, I'm Alex Gilpin. You're new here, and I've never met you and you've never met me, so now you know who I am."

I'm reasonably certain that this was the only introduction like this she ever received. However, this is one instance where Alex may have been the truly appropriate one.

On Thursdays, I pick up Matthew from school to take him to Hebrew class. One particular day, we were experiencing some pretty fierce storms, with violent lightning and thunder. Matthew has always been more than a little unnerved by thunderstorms, so he decided we should go straight home and skip Hebrew class. I reassured him that it would be safe, but he didn't seem convinced.

When we got to his teacher's home, he refused to get out of the car. I tried to urge him, to no avail. His teacher came out of the house, said it was important to have class, and asked him to come in.

Matthew not only refused but made his feelings very clear when he rolled the window down and yelled, "I will not risk my life for Hebrew!"

Sherry Ansher, North Carolina

High-functioning children with autism will often write letters that must be surprising to the outside world. The following correspondence, written by a young man to his teacher and the principal of his school after taking a bus trip, illustrates this point.

DEAR MRS MORRIS AND MRS KOWNACKI, THANK YOU VERY MUCH FOR INCLUDING ME IN YOUR FIELD TRIP TODAY. I LIKED TAUM SAUK MOUNTAIN STATE PARK.
LOVE, JEFFREY

P.S. THANK YOU FOR LETTING ME RIDE RYDER BUS 289. I LIKE GREEN SEATS BETTER SO NEXT TIME SEE IF YOU CAN GET A BUS WITH GREEN SEATS.

Sandy Kownacki, Missouri

Alex was studying history and, as that was my major in college, I was busy meddling or helping (take your pick). We came upon the term "Alien and Sedition Act."

Now, Alex does learn historical terms, but his understanding of the concepts is very limited. Therefore, I asked him if he knew what that act did. He had no clue. So, I explained that it was intended to keep a certain group of people out of the country. I asked him if he knew who they were.

"Lawyers?" was his instant reply.

Alex's idea would have probably been a lot more popular.

My son was placed in a classroom with regular students, without the teacher being informed of his limitations. This omission led her to ask him to leave class, because he was doing "Rain Man imitations."

Author unknown

I've always been a big proponent of inclusion, whenever humanly possible. When Alex was in a preschool group, however, he was in a "special" room with children of all handicaps. One day, I noticed my not-very-verbal son limping badly. The movement led me to check his shoes for a stone. There was no stone, no wound of any kind, no tenderness, and no indication that he had any kind of pain. I was really confused until the next morning, when

I took him to school and saw one of his classmates who had polio. Alex had copied the child's limp perfectly.

I used this story in the next ARD (Admission, Review, and Dismissal) meeting with the school personnel to demonstrate how Alex could learn from and emulate his classmates. I said, "If he can learn this movement so perfectly, just by observation alone, then he can certainly learn behaviors from normally developing children."

That argument helped carry the day, and Alex was permitted to join the rest of the 1st graders in a regular classroom.

———

One of my students, Janice, had a real fondness for a teacher in our building. Every time Miss Lawrence came by, the two exchanged pleasantries, often about dogs—a mutually favorite subject.

It wasn't long before Miss Lawrence got married and became Mrs Zelefron. Janice still called her "Miss Lawrence." So, I wrote a social story to explain the change to Janice. I felt like I had conveyed the concept, but I must have missed a step.

Mrs Zelefron came into the room and, to my delight, Janice called her by the proper name. However, after she left, Janice turned to me and, with a puzzled look, said, "You know what? Mrs Zelefron sure does look like Miss Lawrence."

Ed Nientimp, Pennsylvania

My daughter was bullied by another girl in her class, who teased and taunted her constantly. My regular complaints to her teachers and other school personnel resulted in no relief from the abuse.

One day, as I dropped my daughter off for a visit with my parents, I mentioned the bullying to them, hoping they would have an answer. They seemed concerned, but they did not offer any solutions.

About 1 week later, I received a call from the school to come pick up my daughter, because she was being suspended. I was shocked to hear that, without a word, she had walked right up to the bully, socked her in the face, knocked her out of her chair, and left her crying on the floor.

I picked my daughter up and took her to my parents' home, as I had to go back to work. I didn't want to tell them of her actions, but I did so reluctantly. When I did, my mother looked shocked, but a strange smile came over my dad's face as he said, "Well, sounds like a good fist to the nose fixed *that* problem." It suddenly dawned on me just where my daughter had gotten that idea.

While I do not condone violence, ever since that day, my daughter has never been bothered by that bully again.

Michelle, Illinois

I have a daughter with Asperger's syndrome, who enjoyed school but did not like a particular substitute teacher. In my attempt to be a good parent, I told her that I would pay her a nickel for every positive thing she could tell me about this particular substitute. She was an ongoing sub, so I felt a need to help Jessica find good things about her.

When Jessica returned home from school one day, I asked her if she was able to find anything positive about this teacher whom she clearly did not like. She looked at me for a long time and finally asserted, "Well, she left at noon!"

Jolene Thomas, Idaho

Matt, a young boy with Asperger's syndrome, is a member of the basketball team I coach. I have learned that my "pep talks" do not always affect him as they do the other players, and, often, they clearly don't have the effect I intended. He is always concerned about our winning and trying his best, and he seems bothered when we lose, which I must admit is almost all the time.

We were going into a game, and I said to the group, "This is your team, and this is your game to win or lose." I noticed from Matt's expression that this seemed to make a real impression. I felt pretty proud of making this breakthrough. The game was pretty close, and I could see that Matt was following the game intensely. I realized how "into" it he was when he left the bench to walk out on the floor and, to my shock, gave the signal for a time-out.

I asked him what he was doing. He replied, "You said it was my team, and I decided we needed a time-out!" I told him that the team was my responsibility, and I would decide when time-outs were necessary.

We lost that game by a larger score than usual. However, Matt was very casual and did not seem to be bothered at all. When my wife asked the reason for his new attitude, he said, "Mr Gray is responsible for us losing!"

Brian Gray, Michigan

Ms Smith found one of her students making faces at others on the playground, so she stopped to gently talk to the child. Smiling sweetly, Ms Smith said, "Bobby, when I was a child, I was told that if I made ugly faces, my face would freeze and it would stay like that."

Bobby looked up and replied, "Well, Ms Smith, you can't say you weren't warned."

Autism Advocacy Magazine

My son, Ryan, was struggling with math. Using the logic that had been given to me as a child, I said, "Ryan, you can do it. Math is a piece of cake." He looked up very excitedly and asked, "Cake? Great. Where is it?"

When I explained that there actually was no cake and what I said was just an expression, he lost interest in my explanation and went back to his homework. After working for a while, he looked up at me with sad eyes and shook his head as he said, "Mom, math is definitely not a piece of cake. It's a piece of spinach!"

Allison Woods, Texas

Mrs Rainwater wanted my son John to help her pass out water bottles at school. She asked him to count heads to see how many there were.

He looked around the room intently and then turned with a very puzzled expression as he responded, "Everybody has just one!"

Lindas Contellanos, Georgia

How to Tell a Real Teacher

Real Teachers:

- Grade papers in the car, during commercials, in faculty meetings, in the bathroom, and, when under pressure at the end of a grading period, during church.

- Cannot walk past a line of kids without straightening up the line.

- Are written up in the *Guinness World Records* for the elasticity of their kidneys and bladders.

- Can tell you after 1 week of a new term which parents will show up at Open House.

- Cheer when April 1st does not fall on a school day.

- Have never heard an original excuse.

- Buy Excedrin and Advil at Sam's Club.

- Will eat anything that is put out in the teacher's lounge.

- Have disjointed necks from writing on the blackboard while watching the class.

- Know that secretaries and custodians run the school.

- Hear the heartbeat of a crisis, always have time to listen, and know they teach students, not a class.

Teachers who care about our kids are special in many ways. This poem, written by a parent, illustrates how parents can sometimes feel.

Special Teacher

You held the key that unlocked
The chains of silence
You planted a seed that was nurtured
By the grace of your caring.

These are the doings of the heart
They are not read about or formulated
Although the skill was learned from the
Backbone of text
You have left the harsh lines behind
Solid in technique.

You held out your hand
It was open, safe, and easy to grasp
Your hand opened a door to a new and exciting
World waiting to be explored
You shined a light that caressed the seed
That blossomed into my son.

The world awaits this curious boy
Who was shown the key to grow
You have done your work well
The fruits of your labor are evident in the
Sparkling eye, the smile, and the touch of my boy.

You have done your job well
The seed you tenderly nurtured has taken root
And will now grow, prosper, and be full of joy.

Greg Buckingham, North Carolina

Elvis Lives!

In choosing Alex's senior-year courses, we had one more course to select. With some caution, I chose drama. Alex was willing to go along with it, but he wasn't even sure what they did in a drama class. (To other parents, this was one of the best judgments I made in Alex's education. He responded well and grew because of the experience.)

One day, Alex came home from school with an assignment that struck fear into my heart. The students were to each choose a famous person and act like that person in front of the class, so the rest of the class could guess whom they were impersonating. Alex chose Elvis Presley.

Now, in singing, a child has two challenges. The first is to remember the words, and the second is to sing well. Luckily, Alex remembered words very, very well. However, I was worried that his lack of singing skills would be embarrassing (I'm afraid he inherited his father's voice). I told him that, prior to his presentation, which was scheduled in 3 days, we would choose a different person to impersonate.

The next day, I picked Alex up at school. His drama teacher happened to come by and casually mentioned that Alex had done his performance that day. Evidently a couple of kids were out of class, and Alex's performance had been bumped up. My heart sank as I asked how he did.

The drama teacher said, "Great! Alex walked up to the mike, shook his arms and body slightly, and said, in a deep voice, 'Thank you. Thank you very much.' The whole class screamed out, 'Elvis!'"

Who says kids with autism can't be creative...

Parents Can Say the Dumbest Things

Those who know me well are aware that I am a big proponent of parents/heroes taking an active role in their child's life. I support parents in demanding the best services available to help their child. This activity will naturally take them to the often-dreaded IEP (Individualized Education Program) meeting. I believe parents should be assertive but positive in their service requests. However, sometimes they go too far. These comments were made by well-meaning parents at IEP meetings or, worse, at public events.

———

Temple Grandin was taking questions at the end of a presentation. A lady put her hand up and said, "My son likes playing with cars. How does autism cause that?" For the longest 30 seconds of that woman's life, Temple just stared at her. Then she looked away and said, "Next question."

———

A parent was in her son's IEP meeting and said, "My son seems to resent it when I hit him. Is that because he has autism?"

———

Another mother asked, "My son doesn't like spinach. Will he like it if I call it something else?"

A "very optimistic" mother came up with the idea that her child's school should pay for her to receive personalized Applied Behavioral Analysis training, to be administered by the esteemed Dr Ivar Lovaas, from the University of California at Los Angeles. She wanted to have Dr Lovaas "flown in" so she could receive 40 hours a week of intensive one-on-one training with him, on the school's dime—an estimated $25,000. Before the speechless school personnel could even formulate a response, she added, "Also, who will pay for Dr Lovaas's housing while he is in town for the school year?"

———

A parent stood up when I was speaking and asked me if Alex had ever said curse words. When I replied "No," she said, "Well, if you want to hear some really good cursing, just come over to my house after the presentation." I was unclear as to why she thought I needed that interesting experience.

———

Two parents argued all throughout their child's IEP meeting. Finally, the father stood up and said, "This is your problem! I'm damn sure that no genes from my side of the family had anything to do with this kid's autism!" The room was silent after the father left. The professionals were embarrassed for her and had no idea what to say. Finally, the mother broke the silence and the tension in the room by saying, with a slight smile, "He doesn't know it, but his genes had nothing to do with this kid at all!"

Teachers and School Officials
Can Also Say Dumb Things

Vice principal: "Your son has the cutest red hair and freckles. I just love the time we spend together. I've really come to know your situation very well."
Parent: "My son doesn't have red hair or freckles."
Vice principal (looking puzzled): "Are you sure?"

A school psychologist said, "My years of training and experience in the field assure me that your son has all the characteristics of austis-ism."

Everyone stared at him in disbelief as he ventured, "What's wrong, haven't you heard of austis-ism?"

The school principal stuck his head in the door during a very fractious IEP meeting and wisely offered, "Let me see now—this meeting is supposed to be about helping Jason with his social skills, right?"

After hearing that a child was having sleeping problems, a special-education director turned to the gentleman seated next to the child's mother and asked him if he let the child into bed with him and Mrs Wallace (the mother).

Without blinking an eye, the new school psychologist said, "I doubt that my wife, Mrs Jones, would appreciate it if either the child or Mrs Wallace got into bed with me."

A teacher explained how deeply concerned she was about being able to handle a child with autism in her class the following year. Then she proceeded to fall asleep halfway through the IEP meeting—and snored.

An IEP team leader, upon meeting a parent for the first time, said, "The report says that Pat has been going to the girl's bathroom often during the day. Why do you think he is doing that?"

The mother patiently said, "It may be because Pat is a girl."

A school psychologist offered this monument to educational babble: "It is the professional judgment of this examiner that J—'s lack of ability to function in an independent manner is having a detrimental impact on his functioning independently."

Chapter 6: Home

Even in the sanctity and security of our homes, we are subject to the surprises that our special family members can offer. These anecdotes are fairly typical of how even everyday events can turn into "fun" experiences.

I've always been a pet lover, and I was a little sad that Alex took very little interest in any of our family pets. However, one day I thought that there was a sudden awakening of healthy interest.

I was tossing a rubber ball from the living room out into the hallway (something bachelors can do with impunity) so our very energetic dog, Spencer, could retrieve it—a game he loved. After about five or six tosses, I noticed a real interest in Alex's face as he followed every movement. To my further surprise, he asked if he could do it. I was delighted, and Alex proceeded to throw the ball with some vigor, whizzing the ball past Spencer out into the hallway.

He was successfully throwing the ball, and Spencer was happily bringing it back so he could chase it again. However, after three or four throws, I saw that Alex was bothered and gave a sigh of disgust after each throw. Naturally, I asked him what was wrong.

"What's the problem, Alex?"

"Dad, I keep missing, because Spencer keeps moving his head!"

Poor Spencer thought it was a great game, never realizing that, in Alex's mind, his furry little head was the target.

We were beginning to think our son, Andy, would never get toilet trained. We tried potty books, potty videos, thick training pants, treats, and everything anyone else suggested.

Finally, merely by chance, we bought Andy underwear with his favorite cartoon characters printed on them. This purchase had an unexpected, beneficial effect.

He started urinating in the toilet, muttering all the while, "Don't pee on Barney...can't pee on Barney."

He wasn't completely trained for a long while, though, as evidenced at a public picnic. Andy announced loudly and clearly to everyone in the area, "I pooped in Jurassic Park!"

Jayne Kranc, Indiana

Recently, my son, Steven, complained of having a headache. I brought him into the kitchen and put two Tylenol tablets in his hand. He shook his head and said, "No medicine!" I told him he needed to take the pills to make his boo-boo go away. He then came up with a solution that he thought would take away his headache without ingesting the dreaded pills. He simply held the tablets up against his forehead.

Lucie Beauchesne, Massachusetts

My normally developing son, Ivan, was taking a bath with our son with autism, Eric. I always felt that that Ivan had a minimal understanding of autism, or so I thought. However, during the bath, I heard Eric whining. When I asked why Eric was unhappy, Ivan replied, "I keep washing his hair, and he doesn't like it."

I asked the obvious question, "Then why are you doing it?" He replied with a smile, "Mom, I can't stop. I have 'washing-tism.'" I loved that.

Michele Viteri, Illinois

My son, Joseph, loves to play in the water, so finding him in the backyard with the water hose is not uncommon. One spring afternoon, he was in the backyard happily spraying everything in sight, when I noticed it was starting to rain. In my most urgent mother voice, I said, "Come in right now, it's starting to rain." I went on with what I was doing in another room and returned about 5 minutes later to see if Joseph had, in fact, come in out of the rain.

He came in, all right. He'd also brought the water hose with him and was smiling as he watered the dining room carpet. I had neglected to tell him to leave the water hose outside.

Melanie Kelly, Texas

My son, Jacob, is now a well-behaved and mild-mannered 10-year-old. At the age of 5, however, he was nothing of the sort. One day, I came home to find that our house had been burglarized. As I waited for the police, I held onto Jacob, who did not want to be held because he wanted to run around the yard.

When the police arrived, I brought (or rather, dragged) Jacob into the house so I could speak to the officers. I tried to answer questions as I wrestled with my son. The officers were somewhat bemused at the difficulty I was having with this small child, but they proceeded with their report. Suddenly, Jacob got away from me and, before anyone could move, he lunged at one of the officers and bit him in the stomach. Worse, he didn't let go.

The policeman, who, minutes before, was wondering why I couldn't control this seemingly innocent little boy, was now yelling, "Get him off of me!" I got Jacob by one leg, and the other officer grabbed his other leg as we tried to shake him loose. The policeman was screaming and yelling, dancing around the room with my child attached to his abdomen and two adults attached to the child. I yelled, "Don't hurt him, he doesn't understand!" (I didn't feel that this was the time for an in-depth explanation of autism or the joys of behavioral modification.)

When Jacob let go, the officer's shirt was torn and he was bleeding slightly. The other officer realized that he might be the next target, and he turned to run—but not fast enough. Jacob got him, too—a direct hit on the right buttock. As we attempted to pry him loose, I wondered how the officer was going to explain these marks to his wife.

Both officers left the house in haste. One yelled over his shoulder, "You can come down to the station to file your report. But for God's sake, don't bring *him!*"

Linda Todd, Texas

As with my normally developing daughter, I always said "I love you" to Alex when I tucked him in at night. After a while, he responded in rote fashion, "I love you too."

Being "clever," I said, "But I love you more," to which Alex quickly responded, "Then I love you less."

When my son was younger, he had a pet turtle named David. One day, the turtle burrowed under our neighbor's fence and was unfortunately attacked by their dog. David was retrieved, but he was slightly injured and subsequently became sick. I tried to resuscitate him by taking him to the bathroom and placing him in some water.

The next thing we knew, there was an ambulance on the way to our door. This was the message 911 received from our son: "My mother is in the bathroom with David, who was hurt by the dog and may be dying... there are bubbles coming out of his mouth and we need an ambulance right now!"

He omitted the fact that David was a turtle.

Fortunately, the dispatcher understood (we think), and the ambulance was recalled.

Author unknown, Washington

At an early age, our son wanted very much to purchase tampons. The reason? He remembered an ad that said, "With tampons you can do anything!"

When he first lived on his own, I worked with him to plan and prepare his own meals. For a while, I offered to fix dinner, but breakfast and lunch were up to him. When he went shopping, he returned home and proudly displayed his purchases: a large can of Ultra Slimfast, a quart of milk, and tampons. I already knew why he bought the tampons, but his reasoning for the diet drink was a little confusing until he reminded me of their ad: "A delicious meal for breakfast or lunch."

Author unknown

My husband and I were thrilled when our son with autism, Andy, learned to count. Andy made use of his counting ability time and again, in any way he could. It got a little boring after the 400th time, but we were still pleased with his progress. Then we received our monthly phone bill, with $38 in calls to South Bend, Indiana.

We didn't know anyone in South Bend, but the number was somehow strangely familiar. Then we realized that to dial South Bend from our northwest Indiana home, you need to dial a "1" first. That made the phone number 123456789.

Andy had spent $38 practicing his counting skills every time my back was turned. I tried to call the number to apologize, but it had been disconnected. I can't imagine why.

Jayne Kranc, Indiana

Our family project one Saturday was to scrub the oil marks off our driveway. I'd just gotten started when I had to go back in the house for another bucket of water. When I returned, I found my son, who has autism, scrubbing merrily away, holding his face close to an oil stain and yelling at the top of his lungs. At first I was totally confused, until I noticed the detergent we were using—"Shout."

Author unknown

Our beautiful little girl, Suzie, has autism. When she was about 5 years old, her great-uncle came to visit us at Christmas. He wasn't a terribly sensitive man, as he jutted his thumb at Suzie and said gruffly, "Does she understand anything about Christmas?"

Suzie, who was heavily into self-stimulation at the time, jolted back into our world. Sitting up ramrod straight, she looked him directly in the eye and said defiantly, "Ho, ho, ho."

Suzie and her great-uncle have been the best of friends ever since.

Dennis and Diane, Nebraska

Our son Mitch, who lives in a group home, was visiting for the weekend. He got up in the middle of the night and prepared himself his favorite snack—bread covered with ketchup. Upon hearing Mitch in the kitchen, my husband went in and, speaking somewhat sternly when he saw the ketchup mess, asked Mitch, "What are you doing?!" meaning, "You should not be making this mess!"

Mitch looked at my husband as if to say, "Are you stupid? What I'm doing is obvious," but instead he patiently answered, "I am eating bread and ketchup."

Phyllis-Terri Cold, PhD, New York

About 2 years ago, my husband was struggling to listen to our son express himself on some subject. My son was having a hard time finding the right word, so my husband said, "Spit it out, son!"

This seemed like a strange request to Shawn, but he did it. He stopped talking, spat, and then went back to trying to find the right word.

Sandra Phillips, Virginia

Alex, like most kids, I suppose, continually left his clothes on his bedroom floor. Being a seasoned parent, I delivered a line I had heard from my parents, and one that most of you have probably also heard: "Alex, this is the last time I'm going to tell you to pick up your clothes."

With a sigh of relief, he replied, "That's good, Dad, because I hate it when you tell me that."

To keep my son out of rooms he was obsessed with, we had our doorknobs turned around backward so we could lock the doors easily. This usually worked, until one day, when my daughter and I were both in the bathroom. I heard an ominous click and realized that my son had just mastered a new skill.

Now my daughter and I were locked inside the bathroom, and we could hear my son screeching through the house. Our imaginations ran wild about what was happening on the other side of that door. After 2 very long hours, we were finally freed, only to discover that the kitchen had been ransacked. A gallon of orange juice, an upturned box of cereal, and the contents of our refrigerator were strewn all over the floor. I could have either laughed or cried, but when I saw my son's face, happy and unharmed, I started to laugh.

The next time we went for a relaxing bath, however, we were armed with a telephone and a bathrobe.

Carolyn Scheggia, Pennsylvania

Not too long ago, we were all sitting in the car ready to go somewhere, except for my husband, who was still inside the house. After beeping the horn several times, I asked our son Shawn, who has autism, to go "stick his head in the door" and tell Dad to hurry up.

I looked up a minute later to find Shawn pressing his head into the screen door of the house as he called to his Dad—just like I'd asked him to.

Sandra Phillips, Virginia

Alex's stepdad was encouraging him to go to bed by saying, "Last one in bed is a rotten egg!" to which Alex responded, "Okay, what's the first one?"

I stayed with my nephew, who has autism, while his parents went away on a trip. I had the responsibility of waking him up in the morning, which he didn't appreciate. I shook him gently but firmly and said, "Time to wake up." He attempted to bury his head in the pillow as he groggily replied, "Not wake up. Wake down, wake down."

Marjorie Langhorne, California

After we moved to a new house in a different state, my mother came to visit us. Shortly after she entered the house, our son with autism, who was 3½ years old, got up and walked over to her. "How nice!" we thought. He even took her hand. Terrific—a sign of affection! Then he escorted her right back to the front door and indicated she could leave, as she did not belong here.

We reassured Mother that she was wanted. However, it wasn't long before he took her hand again and walked her into his bedroom, where he left her and closed the door.

Fortunately for my mother, he has done this with us, too...

Robert and Susan Cromwell, Kansas

When John was in high school, one day there was an incident in which he mangled a teacher's eyeglasses. It was, of course, very inappropriate and unacceptable behavior, and it could not be ignored. It seemed right that the teacher should be compensated for a pair of replacement frames. It also didn't seem entirely right that John should get off with no obligations, while his father and I had to pay for his destructive act. He should pay. Yet, his earning power was practically nonexistent—until a snowfall conveniently arrived soon after the incident.

"John," I announced, "you are going to shovel snow because you must pay for those glasses you broke." I showed him the sidewalks that were to be shoveled, and he started in on the task. I was rather surprised at how cooperative and compliant he was. I had expected more resistance to the task. Inside the house, watching him shovel away outside, I felt rather pleased. Not only because

I had done the right thing, but because it was easier than I had expected it to be. Later, I went out to look at the job he had done.

The sidewalks were acceptably cleared. The snow, however, had been piled into a small mountain inside our garage.

Beth Sposato, Nebraska

My little friend Jeff's mother was very concerned about the amount of food their cat was eating, but the cat didn't seem to be gaining any weight. She took the cat to the vet, who informed her that, in fact, the cat was starving.

It wasn't until she replaced the vacuum cleaner bag that the mystery was solved. It turns out that Jeff loved the sound of the cat food being sucked up into the vacuum. This unfortunately explained why the cat's dish was always empty.

One can only wonder what the poor cat must have thought when he saw his food constantly being vacuumed away.

Sandy Kownacki, Missouri

Chapter 7:
Out into the
"Real" World

It is not only necessary, but very important, that parents of children with autism venture out into public with their kids. Trips, whether to the grocery store or to another state, can become much more "exciting" than they are with normally developing children. We're never quite sure how our special kids are going to perceive an event or how the general public is going to react to our kids. The following stories are about some of those adventures.

My son Nicky was usually wary around strangers, so I was very surprised when he perked up and ran over to an insurance salesman that was speaking with me. The salesman was busy telling me how good he is with kids, when my son blew his nose on the man's sleeve and then ran away. Apparently, he just wanted a place to blow his nose. I ended up buying insurance.

Kathy Labosh, Author of *The Child with Autism Learns about Faith*, Pennsylvania

I went shopping with my 14-year-old child with autism, and, as happens with all parents, I "momentarily" lost sight of Sarah. I quickly scanned the parking lot and the surrounding area before returning to the store, wondering if she might be looking for me. There was still no sign of her. Finally, in desperation, I hurried over to the checkout line.

At first I was relieved to see her, but that quickly dissipated as I realized that she was calmly putting her "purchases" on the counter. The cashier was just as calmly ringing up her order. In only a few minutes, Sarah had completely filled a shopping cart with a variety of her favorite items—and had no money to pay for them. I announced to the cashier rather sheepishly that Sarah was my daughter but that these were not my groceries. I apologized profusely and hastily exited the premises with my errant progeny... minus her "wish list" of groceries.

Fisher family, Michigan

———

"What's in a name?" Often, people who are not associated with autism have very interesting interpretations of what autism is. For example, prior to moving to a new school district, I spoke with our new principal over the phone so I could tell her about John's autism. Later, as we completed the routine paperwork, the principal asked, "Just what is an acoustic child?"

In another instance, for a time we considered taking a foreign exchange student into our home. I was concerned about how our potential guest would react to John, so I emphasized his challenges in the information package. I thought this would probably settle the issue, but to my surprise, I received a response several weeks later. The young girl in question was delighted, because she, too, was "artistic."

Beth Sposato, Nebraska

———

Many children with autism "perseverate" or focus on a subject almost to the exclusion of other interests. For too long of a time, Alex focused on bathrooms. That's all he wanted to talk about. One day, while driving in the country, I had about all I could take of toilets, sinks, and urinals. I snapped, "That's it. No more talk of bathrooms for at least an hour. We're going to talk about something else...like that airplane up there."

For a brief moment, Alex looked taken aback. He peered up at the plane, brightened, and said, "Now, Dad, that airplane has wings, seats, and a neat bathroom." Catching my scowl, he added, "I guess you made a mistake by talking about that plane when you knew it had a bathroom on it."

———

When Travis was maybe 4 years old, he kept having nightmares about an "up-hair guy." We could never figure out what he meant by that until one day when we went to the pet store. We were looking at the fish when Travis whispered to me very loudly, "Mom! There is the 'up-hair guy'!!!" His brothers and I looked up at the young man standing near us, who was laughing at Travis's comment. He had a Mohawk!

Jenn Alvey, Utah

Very often, friends can be so absorbed in their own lives that they mistakenly interpret the actions of our children with autism as "normal." This story illustrates that point.

Little-league baseball is a torturous experience for me at best. However, when my normally developing son plays, he wants to see his adoring mother's face cheering him on from the stands. Then there is Darrell, our 10-year-old who has autism. He finds sitting for that length of time difficult, and the constant eruption of noise even more so. About five games into the season, a friend of ours, Bob, sat down to watch the game.

Bob began to tell me how frustrated he was because he had been an accountant for years, and now he was having to look for a job but was unable to find one in his field.

While we were talking, Darrell was playing with the strap of my purse and sucking his tongue.

Bob went on to say that, in his desperation, he took a job in the meat department of a local grocery store.

Darrell was now sliding up and down on the bench. I had a vice grip on him as I tried to be attentive to Bob.

Bob finished his story, "It is incredibly cold back in the meat department. The meat is heavier to carry than you would imagine, and the floors are wet. Someone could slip, and all for minimum wage!"

At that moment, a chuckling sound emerged from Darrell's throat. It grew louder, until he was laughing outright.

In horror at the inappropriateness of it all, I said, "Darrell!"

At which point, Bob took Darrell's hand and said, "That's all right, son. I thought it was a big joke, too. That's why I quit."

Pamela McGee, Georgia

I was driving home with Scott, my typically nonverbal son, from another unpleasant meeting regarding self-abuse and inappropriate behaviors. I had four lanes to cross over to get to the lane I needed. Suddenly, the traffic stopped dead, and I ran into the back of a van. Scott's forehead hit the windshield. He immediately rubbed his head, looked at me, and said, "Oh."

I was so pleased with the fact that he spoke, that I forgot the accident for a moment and said, "So, this is what I have to do to get a word out of you." He continued rubbing his forehead and laughed.

I really want Scott to be verbal. I'm just not sure running into automobiles every day is the best way to make it happen.

Patricia Harman, Ohio

Both of my children with autism were afraid of doctors. Any trip to the doctor was a dreaded experience. One Saturday morning, Jessica had to go to the doctor to have stitches removed. Her brother Richard had to come with us. I assured him that the doctor was not going to look at him—only Jessica.

When the doctor walked into the room, Richard grabbed Jessica and shoved her at the doctor. He wasn't taking any chances that the doctor might be confused and treat the wrong child.

Jennifer Brown, Ohio

When Scott was around 12 years old (and talking in three- and four-word sentences), one of his pleasures was to go to a local lunch place called Dru & Bill's, sit on the same stool as always, and order the same thing he always did— a hamburger with potato chips and a Coke. One day, Scott placed his order and waited to be served as he sat between two other patrons. I turned to talk to

someone else and suddenly heard, "HEY, YOU LITTLE WISE ASS!!!" A man proceeded to grab Scott by the arm with a look of "I'll fix you" on his face.

I jumped up, placed myself between Scott and the irate man, and demanded that he tell me why he was accosting my son. The man said that Scott had reached over, grabbed his hamburger, taken a big bite, and put it back on the plate right under the man's open mouth.

I tried to explain Scott's handicap and offered what I'm sure was Scott's reasoning. "I ordered a hamburger. There's a hamburger. I'll eat that one!" By this time, the man was more composed and understanding. When Scott's hamburger came, I gave it to the man whose hamburger he'd eaten. Scott just went on eating the guy's hamburger, completely oblivious to what was going on around him.

This story has a happy ending, I might add. The man paid for our lunch!

Jean F. Butler, Maine

Four years ago, when my daughter, Julia, was 4 years old, we decided to take a Sunday drive to the picturesque town of Sedona. Julia was finally toilet trained, so we didn't need to bring diapers.

Everything went well on our outing, until we decided it was probably about time to have Julia visit the restroom. We discovered that the restrooms we remembered from our previous trips to Sedona were no longer there. A clerk in a gift shop directed us to the "outhouses" three blocks away.

When we arrived at the outhouse—a new experience for my daughter—I explained to Julia, "You go in here and go potty." She looked a little confused but did as I said. I guess it was my fault for leaving out some important information. Julia stood inside the door and used the bathroom on the floor, fully clothed. I forgot to be more explicit. I neglected to tell her she needed to undress and sit down.

Mary Turnquist, Arizona

At a large family picnic in a local city park, I suddenly discovered that my son Todd, who has autism, had disappeared. He had joined another group of people. A woman was pouring drinks and setting them along the side of a picnic table. As fast as she poured, Todd followed behind her, picking up each cup and drinking the contents. She stopped pouring with an alarmed look on her face.

Todd was waiting for more as I retrieved him, apologized, and returned him to our family picnic.

Vahrlene Crosswhite, Missouri

Our son Ryan is a severely handicapped, low-functioning 17-year-old with autism, and he loves junk food. This story happened about 10 years back.

Ryan's mom and grandma made a quick trip to the market one Saturday afternoon and took him along for the ride. They parked the car directly in front of the store and briefly ran inside to pick up a couple of items, leaving Ryan by himself in the backseat. The storefront was all glass, allowing a perfect view of the car, and the car doors were locked, with Ryan not more than 20 feet away. It was only for a minute or two.

It must have been a very intense motivating factor for Ryan when a lady pulled into the parking space alongside him with several bags of groceries visibly perched on her back seat. We think it was the sack of potato chips protruding out the top of the grocery bag that prompted Ryan to learn how to unlock those car doors. He plunged into the rear seat of the woman's car before she even had a chance to get out. He was "lightning fast" in ripping open that bag and stuffing those chips into his mouth with both hands. When his mom and grandma looked out the store window, they said the expression on that woman's face could never be described, short of capturing it on film.

But certainly, this was no time for pictures. An explanation was going to be tough enough.

Brad Dietz, Michigan

Sometimes the patience of a stranger can be very helpful in an otherwise potentially embarrassing situation.

When our son Loudie was about 7 or 8, I took him to McDonald's for lunch. It was always a challenge to balance a tray of food while holding my infant daughter and trying to manage my flapping, nonverbal son (Loudie has autism).

As I stood at the counter, waiting to order, I was surprised to see Loudie enjoying a Coke, as well as a much-surprised patron who never saw his Coke disappear. Unfortunately, Loudie was hungry as well as thirsty. The next time I glanced over, he was gone. He had planted himself in the lap of an elderly gentleman and was consuming the man's french fries with both hands. I ran over, hastily explaining that my son had a communication problem and that he really didn't understand what he was doing. The elderly gentleman smiled as he responded, "Ma'am, I think he's communicating pretty well. He just looks like a hungry lad to me."

Carolyn Scheggia, Pennsylvania

Many young people with autism have impressive "splinter" skills—an ability to do something in an exceptional way that a normally developing person could never do. This story is about a rather unusual "skill."

Our son Mike is a good-looking young man. A casual observer would never know he has such a severe disability as autism. This is a blessing—most of the time. As with most children with autism, he always had something to perseverate on, and at the age of 12, he caught bees. Remarkably, he could spot one yards away and catch it in flight. He would hold it by its wings, observe it, and then release it and let it fly away. Mike never got stung and rarely hurt the bees.

One day our doorbell rang, and it was the neighbor from down the street. He had just moved in with his wife and mother-in-law. He said, "I don't know about that son of yours!" I responded, "I don't either, but what's he done now?" He fumed that Mike had been peeking in their windows and had really upset his mother-in-law. I looked toward his house and immediately understood. The hedge across the front of his house was in full bloom! I explained that Mike only wanted to catch the bees on the man's flowers and wasn't at all interested in what or who was in the house.

Our new neighbor walked away with a puzzled look on his face—probably thinking there were two strange people living here instead of just one.

Monica Moran, Texas

You know you've been around your child with autism too long when you go to a fast-food restaurant and order a "pink" milkshake. When our son David was a preschooler, he had no difficulty learning his colors, but he could not pronounce words with several syllables. So when we taught him the difference between strawberry (his favorite), chocolate, and vanilla ice cream, he called them "pink," "brown," and "white." David and I thereby developed our own milkshake code, and we had it down pat.

One day on a McDonald's visit, after I'd placed our order, the cashier looked at me blankly and said, "And a pink milkshake?" before it dawned on me what I'd said.

Mothers, you need to get out of the house more often (I know it's not easy) and converse with other adults occasionally.

Lorraine Groom, California

In an attempt to teach my children how important it is to "keep America beautiful," I have been strict to enforce no littering with my son Jeff, who has autism. He enjoys throwing things out the car window.

One day, as we were driving to the mall, much to my surprise, Jeff excitedly said, "I just saw a sign that says it's okay to litter." I assured him that couldn't be true.

He replied, "Yeah, Mom, the sign said, 'Fine for Littering.' It's okay to throw stuff!"

Ann Buckenstaff, Missouri

At the age of 4, Alex was very echolalic and repeated back what-
ever he heard. One day, I took him with me to an IBM computer
exhibition. As we entered the hall, which was loaded with all kinds
of IBM equipment, we were greeted by the quintessential IBM
prototype salesman. He was well trained, perfectly groomed,
and ready for every event—except Alex. No IBM schooling pre-
pared this guy for what he was about to encounter.

Mr John IBM quickly sized us up and, as I'm sure he was
trained to do, said hello to me and directed himself toward Alex,
bending down to his level.

John: "Hello, how are you?"
Alex: "Hello, how are you?"
John: "My name is John, what's yours?"
Alex: "My name is John, what's yours?"
John: "Isn't that neat. We both have the same name."
Alex: "We both have the same name."
John: "Well, John, I'm with IBM and I want to welcome you."
Alex: "I want to welcome you."

A mask fell over John's face—I could tell he was wondering
what in God's name was going on. I just stood there, smiling,
with no intention of resolving anything. This was fun! John tried
another tactic.

John: "Would you like a lollipop?"
Alex: "Would you like a lollipop?"
John: "Well, I have some. I was offering you."
Alex: "I was offering you."
John: "Well, I have some."
Alex: "I have some."

John looked confused and knew that the IBM manual had
failed him.

John: "Well, John, I'll see you around the show."

Alex: "I'll see you around the show."

Numerous times, as I strolled around the hall with my 4-year-old walking recorder, John IBM would go by and sing out, "How you doing, John?" only to hear his words come right back at him. John would smile, sure he was scoring points, and move on. It never dawned on him that there was something else going on.

It was to be a very big day. I was taking my son, James, to see one of the leading Canadian experts in auditory training, Dr Binet. Because I had an appointment with this highly regarded doctor, several of the aides who work with James asked if they could accompany me so  they could meet him. We all excitedly prepared for the big day and drove several hours to Dr Binet's office. Our group of four—the two aides, James, and myself—went in to meet the doctor, somewhat apprehensively. Dr Binet was very gracious. He sensed our nervousness. He spoke to me first and then to the aides, as he asked and answered questions.

Suddenly, he turned to James and said, "Well, young man, we've left you out of the conversation. We'd like to know what you think."

With a perfectly straight face, James told him honestly what was on his mind. He leaned forward and, with better eye contact than he normally exhibits, said, "I think you're fat!" Knowing that the doctor deals with children with autism all the time didn't help subdue my dueling desires to have the ground open up and swallow me whole and to laugh hysterically. Fortunately, neither happened.

Nancy Deaves, Ontario, Canada

While playing miniature golf with a group of individuals with autism, one of the group members began to push his golf ball into the hole with his club, rather than hitting the ball. I said to him, somewhat sternly, "You're cheating!" Without looking up, he said, matter-of-factly, "Men will be men."

Dawn Murphy, Texas

Matthew has always been concerned with health issues. One of our first experiences was with the soft drink "Tab." Matthew's father is a cancer specialist and had mentioned to Matthew that the saccharine in Tab has been linked to bladder cancer in rats. Matthew became very upset because I had told him that I used to drink Tab in my younger days. He seemed reassured when I told him that you had to drink massive amounts of it to be affected. However, a visit to the supermarket revealed that he was still very concerned.

Matthew was reading labels on diet soda bottles when an unfortunate soul picked up a six-pack of Tab right in front of him. He launched into an unsolicited lecture on the health risks of drinking Tab, which he concluded by telling this shopper that she should not buy Tab because she would get bladder cancer and probably die. The woman he was lecturing was shocked and did not seem amused in the slightest. I checked out the vegetables and pretended I didn't know whose child he was.

Matthew also developed a similar perseveration about the health risks of smoking. He approached people who smoked and told them in a loud voice, "Your breath will stink, your teeth will rot, and then you'll die!"

We're not sure there is a future for Matthew as a senator from our state.

Sherry and Mitch Anscher, North Carolina

This year I introduced my 9-year-old son, Matthew, to physical exercise in the form of Tang Soo Do Karate. He takes lessons with a very patient young instructor, Mr Peterson, who encourages children with disabilities to participate. (Besides having autism, Matthew is a below-the-knee amputee.)

One day after class, Mr Peterson told the students that he was taking orders on karate supplies and mentioned to Matt that he might like a pair of rubber nunchucks. Matt asked, "How much do they cost?" Mr Peterson replied, "Five dollars," as he handed Matthew the product list to review.

Matt seemed a little agitated as he reviewed the list. Again, he asked, "How much does it cost?" and got the same reply, five dollars. With that response, Matt was more evidently disturbed and walked away before returning to inform Mr Peterson angrily that he was wrong.

"It is not five dollars. It is only $4.99!"

Esther Udenberg, Minnesota

My son Buz always greets strangers with a friendly "Hi!" It's often funny to watch, as you can see them trying to remember where they met this friendly young man who has just spoken so warmly to them. It gets even funnier when one of the more outgoing strangers answers back, "Well, hello there! How are you doing?" This puzzles Buz, who immediately stymies the stranger by asking intently, "Do I know you?" It's interesting to watch their reactions.

Sandy Grabman, Oklahoma

At about the age of 4, my son became fascinated with pennies and collected them at every opportunity. There was a mall near our home that had a pond, and people couldn't resist throwing coins into it—mostly pennies. It was almost irresistible for my son, so I had to keep a tight rein whenever we were near the pond. However, I did manage to restrain him somewhat with the logic that he couldn't reach his arm into the pond because he might get his clothes wet.

Sometime after I gave him that warning, he and I and his 2-year-old sister went to the mall. As luck would have it, my car wouldn't start when we were ready to leave. I put my two children on the bench near the pond and went just a little distance to the phone to call for assistance. I glanced over a few times as I tried to reach relatives or friends who might be able to come to my rescue, and the children sat quietly and obediently.

The last phone call must have taken longer than I thought. When I turned around again, both kids were off the bench, but their clothes were still there. Sans any clothing, they were happily playing in the water, with my son bringing up a treasure trove of pennies. I had to dash into a store to buy towels to dry them with, while acting like I had no idea whose children were drawing so much attention.

As I came back out, I ran into a friend from school that lived in another town. After saying hello, she began laughing about the two cherubs frolick-ing in the pool with their mother nowhere to be found. Mid-giggle, her eyes dropped down to the towels in my hand, and understanding dawned on her face.

I simply smiled and handed her one of the towels. She willingly helped me with my task. As we dried them off, I suddenly realized that my son had achieved his goal of getting at those pennies without ever getting his clothes wet.

Author unknown, Washington

When Nicholas was 8, he was at the park with his caregiver, Cherie. One minute, he was playing on the swings and the slides. The next minute he was gone, running at top speed as he disappeared over the horizon, just as Cherie caught sight of him. Interestingly, there were three figures on the horizon, not just Nicholas. As Cherie ran to the last point she had seen him, he was nowhere to be found. The only clue was a house with a wide-open door and the sounds of a children's program emanating from it. She knocked on the door and apprehensively went in when there was no response.

There in the living room was Nicholas, contentedly watching his favorite program, as two terrified children huddled together, unsure of who he was and why he had followed them home and taken over their television set. They told Cherie that he hadn't said a single word as he followed them out of the playground, kept pace as they ran home, and helped himself to their hospitality.

After Cherie gave a brief explanation, the children settled down and were relieved to find that they had made a new, but very unusual, friend.

Paul and Coralie Power, Australia

My son tends to focus on several things, but the one that fascinates him the most is women's breasts. It has become such a problem that I literally have to continually tell him, as a well-endowed woman passes by, "Now, mustn't touch, mustn't touch."

A few times I've forgotten, which has resulted in making a few friends and ruining any chance of friendship with some others.

Janice Abernathy, Ohio

Nicholas was enjoying a picnic in the park with his caregiver, Cherie, when he made a hasty decision to visit one of his biggest obsessions—the toilets. Off he went, with Cherie trying to catch him, until he disappeared into the men's locker room area. Arriving too late to catch Nicholas, Cherie watched him disappear not into the bathroom, but into the men's showers.

What was this very attractive young lady to do? Wait and hope everything would be all right, or try to go in to ensure his safety? She chose to tread where not very many young ladies had ever been and ventured into the showers. Almost immediately she stopped dead in her tracks, as she came upon a man taking a shower, singing, as he soaped his body and head with his eyes closed.

She was speechless. If she made any noise, what would this man's reaction be? Fortunately, Nicholas appeared again, running right at her. Clamping her hand tightly over his mouth, she grabbed him and quietly led him out of the shower. The naked man never knew of his "visitors" and continued happily singing away.

Paul and Coralie Power, Australia

When our son was about 5, he demonstrated exceptional skills with locks. We never knew how he did it, but he could quickly open almost any lock. One day we took him to the grocery store, which happened to have a large safe. It immediately drew his attention. I told him to get away from the safe. However, the clerk intervened to say that it was okay for him to play with it, because it was an expensive burglar-proof safe that he couldn't damage. Besides, the clerk said, it would keep him busy while I shopped. This was fine with me.

I think I had just made it through the first aisle when the alarms went off and the huge door of the safe began to swing open. Both the clerk and the store manager stood there with their mouths gaping open. I'm sure the manager was on the phone immediately with the safe company, asking how a 5-year-old child could possibly open their "burglar-proof" safe.

Another time, we lost my son at the Shriner's Circus. I remembered his fascination as he watched the doorway where the animals came in and out. At the time, I assumed he was interested because that was where the animals were kept. As I began to look for him, however, I suddenly realized that it must have been the lock on the door that captured his attention.

Before I could get to the animals' runway, I found him under the control of some very amazed animal keepers, who told me that he had first opened the lock to the animal doorway and then to the big cats' cage!

Fortunately for everyone, the big cats were sleeping and didn't notice that their opportunity for freedom came and went.

Author unknown

Jeff is never satisfied just to look when we go shopping—a tendency I'm sure he shares with many normally developing children. Therefore, when we go out, I have to constantly remind him, "Touch with your eyes, not your hands." A typical child would understand this reproach, even if they don't cooperate. Not the case with my Jeff.

While staying at a motel with a beautifully decorated Christmas tree, Jeff was fascinated with the fragile ornaments. I was afraid that he would break my rule—and the expensive tree decorations. That is, until I came into the lobby to find that he was following my directions and still enjoying the ornaments. Jeff was busy pressing his eye delicately against one pretty bulb after another.

Flo La Roy, Nevada

As a teacher of children with autism, I like to expose them to many different environments. One of their favorite outings is the national park. On one of those trips, I learned to what lengths one of my students would go to acquire his favorite treat.

We were ready to play volleyball when I realized that an important component was missing: the ball. It had been there just a moment ago, so one of my darlings had obviously hidden it away somewhere. I encouraged the culprit to bring it back and spoke to them all about how the entire group couldn't play if we didn't find the ball. No ball appeared. I threatened—gently, of course—and even pleaded, to no avail. Finally, I knew that most of them really liked sweets, so I offered a prize to the person who "found" the ball. That got them interested, and they all scurried away, looking everywhere.

After 10 minutes of searching, there was still no ball, and we were now also missing one camper. We staff members began looking and, after a few minutes, heard a seemingly far-off voice. We couldn't place it—up in the trees or down around the bushes? We just kept following the cries of "Help, help." We were confused, because in the area we were drawn to, the cries of "Help" strangely did not seem to come from ground level. Then I saw a fellow staff member's chin drop as she pointed at—of all places—the outhouse.

We were really glad to find our wayward charge but were dismayed to discover where he was. His voice was coming not from the commode area but from *under the outhouse*. As we held our noses and peered down into the commode pit, we saw him standing up to his hips in indescribable filth—proudly holding the volleyball.

After we drew straws to see who would reach down and pull him up, he was rushed (and I mean rushed) to the nearby lake and given a quick bath while he held on to the volleyball—the key to securing his prize.

Author unknown

In his book, *Soon Will Come the Light*, Thomas A. McKean tells of an air flight with some airline personnel who were unfamiliar with autism. It seems that one of his friends had casually told the ramp agent of Thomas's autism. Showing a great deal of concern, but an abundance of ignorance about the condition, the airline personnel surrounded this very high-functioning author as he began his trip. They checked on him every 3 minutes for fear he might try to either hijack the plane to parts unknown or become physically unruly during the flight.

Unfortunately for the flight attendants, there was a stopover, and Thomas had to get off the plane, supposedly under the control of one of the ground personnel. When the agent turned his back to answer another passenger's question, Thomas decided he'd had enough of this unnecessary overprotection and exited stage left to explore the airport.

When they realized he was missing, they (and we're not making this up) put out an all-points bulletin to find this strange person with autism. However, Thomas showed up on his own after an hour-long traverse of the airport. As he strolled up, eating an ice cream cone and carrying his favorite teddy bear, the security guard grabbed Thomas and screamed into his walkie-talkie, "Target is secure—I repeat—target is secure."

Never having been a "target" before, Thomas tried to make up by offering the staffers some of his ice cream and an opportunity to read his poetry.

Like many young teenagers, Alex sometimes needed to be re-minded about common courtesies. This led to my son bringing me up short yet again. We were about to step into an elevator with two other ladies. My 6-foot son almost knocked one of them down as he barged onto the elevator. I reproached him and told him he should always let ladies go first on elevators or through doors. He looked confused but said "okay."

About 1 week later, it happened again as we entered a building. He moved ahead of—or should I say through—three women who were about to walk through a large door. I gave him the same admonition. Again, he looked perplexed, so I asked why he was confused. He said, "Dad, you said that women and men are supposed to be equal. So why do we have to hold doors for them?"

As is the problem with most high-functioning teenagers with autism, my son does not have the social graces or sensitivity that we would like. This couldn't have been more obvious than when a girl asked him to go to the school dance! We were delighted!

However, upon being invited, my less-than-tactful son replied that he wanted to go but his dad didn't have a car big enough for the girl—who was overweight—to fit into. Needless to say, there was no date.

Author unknown, Washington

Alex did not have the best sense of social interaction—particularly regarding the often-confusing world of dating. My efforts to clarify things led to this conversation:

"Alex, do you think you'd like to go out on a date?"

"What's a date?"

*"Well, it's where you go to a movie or a play or to the park
with someone you like, enjoy being with, and care about."*

"Yes, I'd like to do that. Yes, I'd like that!"

"Who do you think you'd like to go with, someone at school?"

"No, Earl Collins."

*It was clear that we were on two different wavelengths. I
was thinking of a few girls who smiled and spoke to Alex, and he
was thinking of Earl Collins, who is a nice guy, but is one of my
friends and is 55 years old. However, when I think about it, Earl
did meet the criteria I gave to Alex as I explained what dating
was all about.*

———

My son will watch a movie, pick up on a few lines, and repeat them
time and time again. Recently, we saw "Pretty Woman" and, for
whatever reason, an unfortunate line stuck in his head.

I should tell you that my son is in his early 20s. He's a good-
looking fellow who appears very normal and stands over 6 feet tall.

We went to a fast-food restaurant for lunch. It was very crowd-
ed and had several lines of customers. In the line next to us stood
a very nice couple. My son looked at the gentleman, who nodded
pleasantly and smiled. Just then—to my horror—the line from
"Pretty Woman" popped out: "That'll be fifty bucks, mister, and
for seventy-five, the wife can watch."

The shock and anger this comment created led me to think our
son was going to be socked in the jaw. However, I quickly intervened and convinced the gentleman that it was not personal.

All the same, I noticed that couple didn't choose to sit next to
us in the restaurant.

Author unknown

One of Alex's less-than-polished social skills was introductions. I'm sure this had to do with his inability to understand relationships.

Nevertheless, I felt that a little training could help. Whenever we met one of his classmates in a mall, or wherever, he barely acknowledged them, and I might as well as have been a nearby bench, in terms of Alex introducing me. So, we had our lessons.

One day we met one of Alex's classmates, who happened to be Asian and one of the brightest students in his grade. "Dad, this is someone from my school," he said (not great, but an improvement). "This is my Dad." (Not bad.)

I reached out my hand to meet this gracious young lady as Alex added, "Her name is Dao Ming Chang—isn't that a silly, funny name, Dad?"

We had a little more work to do on introductions.

In an effort to get Matthew more involved with his peers, I encouraged him to follow Atlantic Coast Conference basketball—a near religion in our part of the country. He quickly became focused, or you could say perseverated, on Duke and loathed their archrival, the University of North Carolina (UNC).

One Christmas, Matthew received a Super Nintendo basketball game in which you could choose names for your two competitors.

Naturally, he chose his most- and least-favorite teams. A typical half-time score was Duke 150, UNC 0. One day, some adult friends of ours borrowed the game and thought it would be humorous to change all the scores so UNC appeared to be creaming Duke.

After the game was returned, we heard a bellow of dismay from Matthew's room. He came stomping out and told us what had happened. We realized how seriously he took this grievous offense when he said we should never speak to those friends again.

He dramatized his feelings by pointing his finger in the air and, using a phrase we can only assume he heard during the evening news, said, "We must sever all ties!"

Fortunately, in time, he forgot his edict and was able to interact with our friends once again.

Sherry and Mitch Anscher, North Carolina

One day, my daughter Jennifer was speaking to Alex when he casually announced that he had to call a girl after they finished talking. She was pleasantly surprised at this venture into the "social world."

The following conversation ensued.

"Alex, you're calling a girl? That's great, but why?"

"She is in my social skills class and she gave me her number and asked me to call her. I don't know why."

"Well, what will you talk about?"

"I will just let her talk. It was her idea."

"Well, Alex, is she a girlfriend?" Jennifer asked, hope surging through her mind.

"Yes, I guess so. She is a girl, and she is a friend."

Disappointed but undaunted, Jennifer asked if he would like to have a real girlfriend. Alex was unclear as to what she meant, so Jennifer explained that a girlfriend was a person you would go out with on a regular basis and do things with all the time.

Alex said that sounded good and that he would like very much to have a girlfriend. Jennifer was feeling that a really special communication with Alex had just transpired. Then Alex continued, "How about you, Jennifer? Do you have a girlfriend?"

Ashley, my 12-year-old daughter with Asperger's, was explaining to our 9-year-old the art of getting a boy to be interested in you. Ashley offered this wisdom to her wide-eyed sibling: "First, you look away when he stares at you. Then, you blink your eyes at him. But, if you really want him to know that you are serious, you talk about marriage and children."

Kim Hammers, Texas

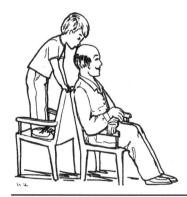 My 9-year-old son with autism developed a penchant for bald heads, for reasons that were never clear. Any bald head was very interesting to him. However, I didn't know how interesting until one day when we were at a public function.

I went to get a drink of water for the two of us. When I turned around, he was surprising some nice gentleman by standing on a chair behind him and affectionately kissing his bald head.

The expression on the man's face was priceless. Thankfully, after some explanation, he was also very understanding.

Author unknown

My son Scott is a young adult with autism, who is doing very well. He lives largely independently, and I am very proud of him. I refer to him as a delightful combination of Rain Man and Forrest Gump.

To prepare this special man for the world, I drilled as many manners into him as he could possibly stand. I included admonitions about certain situations that indicate he should be cautious.

One of these was my warning that most adults—particularly women—don't like to discuss their age. However, this training fell by the wayside when he met a woman and they had the following conversation:

Scott: "You are a very pretty lady."

Christy: "Thank you, Scott."

Scott: "Do you mind if I ask you how old you are?"

Christy: "Well, that is a subject I think we can avoid."

Remembering (somewhat) his training, Scott recognized that he had ventured onto forbidden ground. However, his response was classic Scott.

Scott: "Oh, I get it—that means you are really old, huh??"

Mrs Lambeth, North Carolina

My daughter Alison is focused on health and will discuss it any time. However, she tends to offer well-meaning counsel to some who may not appreciate it.

One day, Alison accompanied me to a gym. After working out, we went into the locker room. I didn't notice she had wandered into the shower area. There was a very heavy lady in the shower, lathered up with soap and shampoo. Alison said, "Do you know you're fat?"

Before the shocked woman could respond, Alison added, "But, if you will eat salads or other low-calorie foods and exercise, you will be thinner and have much better health."

Dr Jeanie McAfee, California

Those with autism that are higher functioning often have interesting interactions with business personnel, particularly when they write letters. This is a letter to a company with which many of you may have had dealings.

Dear Columbia House,
Buying these 12 tapes plus the other eight means I must pay $89.70.

I understand that I can buy these eight tapes within 3 years. If you make me pay any more than the stated amount, so God help me, I'll sue.

Sincerely,
Allison Daggett

P.S. After this, I'm canceling my membership.
P.S.S. Even though I'm only 12, you'd better take me seriously.

Diana Daggett, New Mexico

Politics

Our political structure is not always completely understood by those with autism. The following two stories offer an interesting view on politics.

—————

My 29-year-old son Chris has always had compulsions regarding government, dates, and presidents. He knows all the presidents' names and the dates of their terms in office. He insists on voting each year and spends days and months considering his choices.

I think the list he made for himself for the 1998 election is self-explanatory and amusing, especially his reluctance to vote for a woman:

1998 Primary

- I will only vote for president.
- I will vote for a man if possible, even if nasty.
- Among the men, I will vote for a nice candidate.
- I favor Gary Heart. *[sic]*
- I will see if there is anyone that I like better than Gary Heart.
- I will put the candidates in order.
- If possible, I will vote for someone better than Gary Heart.
- If possible, I will vote for someone of my dreams.

Carol H. Benjamin, Virginia

Dear Senator Domenici,

I'm asking you to clean up New Mexico. I'm a 5th grader in Mrs Kline's Class. My name is Allison Daggett. I think the WIPP project should be abolished and that you should work to clean the air. I also think that more solar power plants should be put in New Mexico.

You should try to get people to stop throwing trash around and start recycling. To make a long story short, I want you to clean up.

Seriously,
Allison

P.S. You can call my mom at 555-1212.

Diana Daggett, New Mexico

Chapter 8:
Sexual and/
or "Improper"
Language

O ur loved ones with autism are often bemused and unimpressed by our preoccupation with sex and "improper" language.

My husband and I were making love when we suddenly realized that our 13-year-old son with autism (Dan) had quietly opened the door and was watching with a seemingly confused look on his face. We were both shocked and very concerned about Dan's reaction. Hurriedly putting on my robe, I went to see Dan, who had gone into the kitchen and was making a sandwich. I attempted to engage him in a conversation about what happened.

"Dan, are you okay?"

"Yes." (He continued making his sandwich.)

"I want to tell you that Mother and Dad love each other and what you saw was one way we show it."

"Okay." I didn't think his "okay" matched my anxiety level, so I continued.

"In fact, Dan, that's how we made you...by our love."

"Okay." (No expression.)

I still felt like I wasn't getting through, and, not knowing how to proceed, I asked a leading question.

"Do you think you'd like to do that one day? Show love like that?"

Shaking his head and, with a sigh, he responded, "Nope...looks too much like hard work!"

(Name withheld at mother's request)

My daughter Anne Marie's father and I divorced, and several years after the divorce, I remarried. My new husband was scheduled to be in the town where Anne Marie attended school, so I asked him to drive her home for Thanksgiving holiday. I thought this would give them a chance to become better acquainted.

As they began the trip, Anne Marie turned to him and calmly said, "Bill, I think you should know that Mother does not like sex." He replied that he certainly wouldn't want to do anything to upset me. And, although he tried to appear calm, he soon found he was lost and had driven 10 miles out of his way.

Margaret Pothoff, California

At the age of about 9 or 10, Alex was very immodest about keeping his clothes on. He just couldn't figure out why there was so much fuss about wearing clothes, if you felt good without them. One day, we were at a suite-motel and were all dressing, except for Alex, who was stark naked. When the maid came to the door, Alex opened it and just stood there, looking at her blankly. She stared back. Finally, Alex said, in his curiously naive manner, "Do you want something?"

I noted that the maid did not come back to clean our suite for the rest of our stay.

As my brother Jimmy entered his teens, my dad realized that it was time to talk to him about going through puberty. Dad sat Jimmy down for a "the talk" and started out by saying, "Jimmy, soon you'll become a man." That's as far as he got before Jimmy cut him short, saying, "I don't want to be a man. I want to stay a little boy forever." He then got up, walked away, and wouldn't discuss the matter any further.

My mom's response? "Most of them feel the same—Jimmy's just more honest than most."

Jennifer McIlwee Myers, Aspie At Large and author of
How to Teach Life Skills to Kids with Autism and
***Asperger's*, California**

I was watching a classic movie, the remake of *I Was a Teenage Werewolf*, with my son who has autism. One of the characters suddenly spoke of scaring someone so bad that they "lost control of their bodily functions." Apprehensively, I asked him if he had any idea what that meant.

Without missing a beat or taking his eyes from the screen, he said, "Rusty zipper—yellow socks."

Mary Ann Coppola, New York

When Robert was learning about opposites and contrasts, I prompted him to say, "This is boy, not girl," "This is hot, not cold," and so on. He picked up on this quite well, and we do it often, much like a game.

One morning, I was fixing breakfast for Robert. I automatically started differentiating, "This is regular toast, not French toast."

Some days later, I was snoozing and Robert woke me up with a kiss on my cheek. He rubbed his nose and mouth on my cheek much longer than usual, so I mumbled, "Just regular kiss, Robert."

He mumbled back as he continued to kiss me, "Just regular kiss, not French kiss." I woke up real fast! For a minute, I was stunned. Who in God's name could have taught him about "French kiss"? Then, after a long and agonizing moment, I felt great relief as I remembered the lesson about French toast. Whew...

Norma Page, California

I think one of the funniest things my 6-year-old son with autism, J.J., has done happened during a trip to the mountains.

We had checked into a motel and decided to go for a swim. After getting out of the pool and going back to the room, I undressed J.J. to change him into dry clothes. No sooner had I turned my head than he made a mad dash for the door and ran down the hall naked. Seeing the door of another room slightly open, he swung it open, disappeared inside, and immediately started jumping up and down on the bed—laughing and stark naked.

The lady in that room was getting ready for dinner and came out of the bathroom in her slip to join her husband, who had been down the hall getting ice. In absolute shock, they watched this naked stranger-child, who hadn't been there seconds before, frolicking on their bed. The look on their faces is something I won't ever forget. I'd never laughed so hard.

Autism sure can have its funny moments!

Debbie Bedard, New Hampshire

My teenage son not only "appears" to be normal, but immodestly I say (with much input from others) that he is also a very good-looking young man.

However, he can very definitely act like someone with autism. This contrast led to a very interesting interaction. We went grocery shopping and proceeded to the checkout counter. The young lady ringing up our purchases was very obviously impressed with this tall, strapping young man and kept glancing his way as she rang up our bill. Since she didn't get a reaction, she gave him a cute smile and, flirting with her eyes, said, "How are you today?"

He snapped back from wherever he was, looked directly at her, and said enthusiastically, "Wednesday, I'm going to take a bath!"

Her mouth dropped open in stunned silence. He was satisfied with his response, and I smiled and exited stage left as fast as possible. I still smile every time I think of her startled look.

Dottie Jurgens, Texas

Years ago, my daughter brought home her new husband to visit us for the first time. We were sitting in the living room getting acquainted, when there was a loud "pop" in the next room. I, knowing what had happened, tried to ignore the noise and draw no attention to Peter. However, my son-in-law still looked concerned and asked what had happened. I tried again to defer, but he was persistent. I reluctantly explained that our son Peter had learned the day before that if he climbed up onto the end of the sofa, he could pee on the electric light bulb in the table lamp with astounding results and a wonderful explosion.

Our newest family member looked for all the world like he wished he hadn't asked.

Elizabeth Hirsch, New Mexico

My daughter Anne Marie told me one day that she intended to never marry or have a boyfriend. She firmly stated, "I guess you can just say, 'Anne Marie's my name, and chastity's my game'."

Margaret Pothoff, California

My husband and I recently took our daughter with autism to visit another branch of our family. This was a somewhat stressful visit, for two reasons. First, it was at the home of the very "proper" matriarch of our family—our great aunt. Second, this segment of the family had suggested that there really wasn't anything wrong with Beth that couldn't be worked out by handling her a little more strictly.

Beth's appearance that day did nothing to allay that idea. She was dressed neatly and quietly assumed her place in the living room, where we all sat around our aunt. All the proper conversation ensued, until Beth put her hand in the air and, in perfect diction, said, "Where is the goddamned bathroom?"

(The first thought that ran through my mind, in our defense, was that everyone present knew my husband never talked like that. Unfortunately, this narrowed the options considerably as to where she had heard this language.)

I quickly interceded with, "Beth, the gosh-darned bathroom is right down the gosh-darned hall, dear."

Everyone ignored her outburst, and I never again had to listen to the family's insistence that Beth was entirely typical.

Susan Moreno, Illinois

While our 32-year-old son, Mitch, was visiting us at home, I asked him, "Is there anything else I can do to help you?" Like most parents, I should tell you I've left no stone unturned to give Mitch all we can, so I was surprised by his answer: "Take better care of me."

I felt a little guilty and confused, so I asked, "Son, what would you like me to do?"

Looking very serious, Mitch replied, "Get me girls to go to bed with."

I was speechless. I did the best I could with the situation by saying, "Maybe someday in the future."

Thankfully, he accepted that answer.

Phyllis-Terri Gold, PhD, New York

Not only do I have a daughter with autism, but I teach students who have autism, as well. One of them, Jeff, is very unpredictable and a real "free thinker." Recently, while walking down the hall with a concerned look, to no one in particular Jeff blurted out, "I sure hope my penis is okay!"

Sandy Kownacki, Missouri

For several weeks, we had an unusual occurrence in that the pilot light in our clothes dryer was always going out. I constantly found it inoperative. It was a real puzzle. Finally, we discovered that our son John, who stands at just the right height, was putting the pilot light out in a very "unique" way.

Our first clue was that John wasn't asking to go to the bathroom quite as much as usual.

Beth Sposato, Nebraska

My 14-year-old daughter was having a party with her very "proper" friends. Everyone was trying to act grown up and adult-like. Suddenly, her brother Jeremy ventured onto the scene. Jeremy has autism and was going through the challenges of puberty at the time. He noticed that one of her male guests had a large amount of hair on his arm. Since he was impressed with this guest's hair, he assumed that the interest would be reciprocated.

With no warning, he dropped his pants and displayed to everyone present the four new hairs he had grown, pointing them out for everyone to see. My red-faced daughter was sure that the disgrace and humiliation she experienced in front of her peers meant the end of her social existence for at least 25 years. However, I imagine the attendees will never forget *that* party!

Since that day, Jeremy has to be watched closely because he will proudly show off his new "hairs" to anyone who mentions the word—including the mailman who has a moustache, the school principal (who, on the first day of school, made the innocent mistake of complimenting Jeremy on his combed hair), and the very surprised UPS lady in short sleeves, who had had noticeable hair on her arms.

It may not be right for a parent to get any satisfaction in the shock of a perfectly nice person, but if you could have only seen their faces...

Sandra Joyce, Pennsylvania

Chapter 9:
The Workplace

E very day, more young men and women with autism are being introduced into the workplace. The combination of our young people with the propriety of the business world can result in some very humorous situations.

My son Mike got his first job in the real world in his mid-20s. We were all pleased that he was able to adapt, and the employees were accepting of his less-than-normal work habits, such as refusing to lick or even wet envelopes to close them but instead sealing them all with packing tape. One day, his supervisor's boss came in and turned out the overhead light that lit both his office and the area where Mike was working. He quickly turned on a lamp so Mike could work and told him that it would only be about 5 minutes before he turned the light back on. He explained that he needed the light off to be able to see a computer screen in his office.

The big boss answered the phone and handled various interruptions while he reviewed the screen in his office. Finally, with all of that out of the way, he turned to the screen in the darkened room, only to have his office lit up without warning.

He turned to chastise the offender who had turned the light on. There stood Mike, pointing to his watch and saying, "Five minutes—your time is up!"

Anita Ferman, Texas

My son was in a job-training program that led him to work in a local grocery store. He performed several of the jobs there, one of which was cashier. Once he learned his duties, he did a pretty decent job. However, his "seeing the world exactly as it is" led to an interesting situation.

He was checking out a customer who obviously didn't value honesty very highly. He tried a trick that other petty thieves have pulled off easily on young people who work the cash register. As he neared the counter, he put two items on the moving belt and another two under his jacket.

My son hardly even glanced at him as he rang up not two but four items. The customer complained about the "overcharge." My son matter-of-factly informed the gentleman that he had also rung up the two items he was hiding under his coat. The would-be thief exited as rapidly as possible.

We found this interesting because even though our son appears so unaware, he is often acutely aware of what is going on around him—even when he gives the impression that he doesn't have a clue.

Author unknown

I made the tough decision to give up my job as an editor to devote my time and energies to our daughter with autism, Maureen. Obviously, I had to tell my boss, Mr Bumble. This is a gentleman who, at least in his own mind, is a legend in the media world.

He was definitely also the kind of man who doesn't like losing. It was certain that he would not like losing his editor, right-hand man, and heir apparent.

I went into great detail as I explained about Maureen and how she needed nonstop, minute-to-minute attention from someone with a tremendous amount of energy and strength. She required someone who could work with her endlessly—hour after hour—with a truckload of patience.

At first Mr Bumble seemed to understand. He nodded his head and seemed deep in thought. However, I soon realized that his thought process was not one of sympathy but of seeking inventive ways to keep me. I could work at night, on the commuter train, when she slept, when I slept, and the like. Mr Bumble's ideas were definitely getting weird. I tried hard to stay flexible but, clearly, my days working on his magazine were over. Still, he kept talking, and I kept giving the same answers and the same reasons, explaining time and again how difficult and demanding this challenge was going to be. Finally, after he had just about ground me down to a fine white powder, he gave in (or so I thought) and admitted that I would have to look after Maureen full time. Then he gazed off into space for a long time before turning back to me and saying (I swear this is true), "Well you know, Joe, it doesn't have to be all bad. I mean, maybe you could do something productive with all that free time and write a book or something."

Joe McKeon

I often have the responsibility of going out to speak to members of the general community, particularly in relation to placing some of our clients with autism in jobs.

Recently, I went to a factory in an area of Trenton that is predominantly Polish. I launched into my explanation of autism and emphasized that supervisors have to be concrete in their directions. For instance, they should say "Move faster" if they want a client to increase his or her speed. I warned that an urging of "Move it along" could cause everything on the desk to be placed on the floor or some other "interesting" interpretation.

One lady, who was a supervisor, raised her hand and offered an analogy that caught me way off guard. "So, it's just like being Polish!" she said. My mind searched wildly for her meaning. Was I about to be hit with a Polish joke in this environment? Did she totally misunderstand my explanations?

Finally, after what seemed an eternity, she added, "You see, a lot of the people here don't speak very much English, so I have to be very clear, and it always works better if I *show* them what to do, rather than *tell* them."

I doubt if this woman had very much formal training in behavioral management or education, but she certainly taught me something that day. Now I talk about visual cues in all my presentations.

Peter Gerhardt, New Jersey

My brother, David Sudbury, is high functioning but still definitely offers some very "autism-specific" behaviors. Recently, he got a job (he's had many) where he works in a print and reproduction room. Things were going reasonably well until the president of the company noticed some very unusual mail coming to their address.

The mail was not addressed to their company—Smith and Martin—but rather to "Smith and Sudbury," attention of David Sudbury, vice president. It seems David had changed the company name to a more "appropriate" title and had appointed himself to an executive position in the process. He was happily directing things to be accomplished that he felt were best.

The president was furious and stormed into David's area, waving a piece of the "creative" stationary in his hand. He found David in the middle of a copying project. The boss exploded as he stammered, "Give me one reason why I should not fire you right now!"

David very calmly answered, "Because I'm working on this project at the moment."

As you may imagine, he no longer works for Smith and Martin, or, for that matter, Smith and Sudbury.

Donna Lane, Florida

Having a person with autism in your workplace has many positives, and I often tell people that. Mike has had a genuine impact on our office in many ways. One is that he has changed our ritual of having birthday parties.

One year it came time for his party, and I told him to come into the conference room, as we were going to sing "Happy Birthday" to him. To my surprise, he refused. When I asked him why, he replied that we couldn't sing because his birthday was actually the previous Saturday, and this was Monday. He was adamant.

I thought for a little while and asked him if it was okay if we sang "Happy Birthday, last Saturday." He smiled and said that would be just fine.

Since then, whenever anyone has a birthday on a weekend, we always add in the appropriate day. It was really fun when one person had their birthday while on vacation and we had to sing, "Happy Birthday, Tuesday before last."

Annette Vick, Texas

I was quite proud of Alex when he worked with me at the Autism Society of America (ASA) conference in San Diego. I taught him how to sell the conference proceedings manual. He had learned the important factors of the book very well and related them to everyone who came near the table. He handled money and credit card machines, helped with inventory, and the like.

A woman showed up at the table specifically to speak to Alex. It was endearing as she said, "Alex, I saw you at the ASA conference in North Carolina, when you sang 'You'll Never Walk Alone' at the closing of the conference. It was one of the most dramatic moments of my life, and I had tears of joy in my eyes for an hour after you spoke. I just wanted to meet you and tell you what that meant to me."

Alex looked at her and, without missing a beat, said, "So, do you want to buy a book?"

One of our coworkers has autism and has somewhat latched onto me to be his guide at work. One day he came in and accurately described why he was late for work: "My buzz-buzz clock did not buzz-buzz."

He also overheard a few of us talking about beer and seemed to want to be in on the conversation—something he rarely does. I asked him what kind of a beer man he was and he replied, "I am an ice-water–type beer man."

Mike also hates bugs and brought my attention to a problem in his area by drawing in great detail how the rug and lamp would look with bugs on them. He even drew creases in the rug. When asked what they were, he said he had to add those because bugs could be hiding in there.

He came to work and asked me to look in his hair because he had passed under a tree. He asked me to examine his head to see if a twig, branch, or limb had fallen into his hair.

Annette Vick, Texas

There is a delightful young man with autism who works in our office. He is a workplace treasure because he enjoys doing the things that everyone else hates, like stuffing envelopes. Recently, he worked a few more hours than usual, and I gave him a little bonus. This caused him to write the following letter to "yours truly":

Dear Wayne, [It took about 4 years for him to call me "Wayne," as I was always just "The Boss."]
Thanks so very much for when the last time I was paid. I was paid one hundred and fifty dollars and sixty-six cents. Yes. $150.66. That made me feel really happy because that was so much more of a good amount of money for me to be paid for.

Your most loyal and favorite employee,
Mike

———

Recently, when I was leaving a company for another opportunity, I was going around giving hugs to most of the office staff. However, when I came to a coworker who has autism, I reached out my hand. He looked at me and said, "I'm sorry, but I cannot touch your hand because you have been eating a bagel. But, I can do this."

With that, he stood up from his chair, walked around behind me, and patted me on the back like a child.

Jennifer Gilpin Yacio, Texas

Letters from Mike

The following are letters from "Future Horizons' most favorite and #1 employee," Mike. As you may suspect, Mike has autism. We have left his writing exactly as it is in his letters. This will give you an idea of Mike's effusive and endearing, though not always grammatically correct, perspective. Enjoy!

What Mike Did on His Birthday in 2011

Dear Teresa Corey,

Hi friend. Or if you prefer about me saying hi to you in another way like hi Teresa. You like that better? Well anyway, I finally wrote a letter like this to you for 1 reason and that was you wanted me to write to you to tell you about how my 2011 birthday went.

Well the first thing that I did on my 2011 birthday was grooming. And so I was cutting nose hairs off from my nose if there were any with a tiny pair of scissors. And after that I shaved my face with shaving cream along with a razor.

And after grooming I went to my parents' house and had a birthday breakfast meaning I had eats at their house.

I had to hurry up fast to have my birthday breakfast of eats so that me and my mother could start to have our fun out as soon as possible. So me and my mom went out for fun as soon as possible like planned. We headed to Fort Worth together to go to The Cowgirl Hall of Fame Museum like we went there before on another one of my birthdays.

After me and my mom getting to The Cowgirl Hall of Fame Museum we went to a small theater downstairs to see an 8-minute feature of something I do not know what on a big screen.

Then we had presents. And we had a pumpkin pie as the birthday dessert. I had it with a milk and a half. The birthday dessert was not things like cookies or cake or candy or chocolates or candy bars or popsicles and or beverages like soda pops and or root beers. I gave up on those too. I eat and drink natural things.

You want to know how old I am now? Okay, I have you know I am 42 years old now. Yes. 42. I have 8 more times left for me to be in my 40's. So with me 42 years old, how many birthdays do you think I have had? Take a guess. 42. Right? I think you knew that anyway, did you? Sure. A person like you would be in your 50's. If you are 52 or 53 or 54 or some other age in your 50's.

There friend. That is my story written to you about what kinds of goings on in my 2011 birthday. It was only an okay birthday. And Teresa, let me have you know about that before your 2011 New Years Eve day birthday. If you can get 5 birthday cards from me for your 2011 New Years Eve day birthday. Because 5 is your favorite number is it not?

This letter to you from me is nearly finished. So this letter to you from me will be written to you goodbye now and that I should have 5 good birthday cards to give to you.

Sincerely,
Mike P. Ferman

Mike's View on Vacations and Hawaii

Dear Teresa Corey,

Hiya Teresa. It is written in this letter to tell you that first of all, there is really this time a regular ordinary normal letter. You really are very happy to get my letter that tells all about my 2011 birthday. And there is questions being answered to you in this letter I think along with some comments in this letter too.

Now the reason I do not like to take vacations anymore is because me and my mom and my dad and their pet dog named Precious have sometimes got some bad people around our own suburban area where we live in that I really like very much, if I go out of town with somebody like my mom, I worry that some bad person can come to our address and break into my back yard house and try to steal some certain specific belongings of mine whatever they are that I really love very much and that bad person try to take these certain specific belongings of mine out of my back yard house and try to get them ruined.

I really like being around my belongings in my back yard house very much as I can every day so that I can look after them all the time.

Now I also know that you have been to Hawaii. I have always never been to Hawaii all my life. But I know a few things about Hawaii. Like Hawaii is a hotspot meaning sunspot place like other hotspot meaning sunspot places. Filled with island girls, warm beaches, nightclubs, and things to do in the sea like sailing, surfing, water skiing, snorkeling, and scuba diving.

When you had to go to Hawaii for work you could not possibly have really had a home in Hawaii, did you? What are you talking about this pig that Hawaiian people at this luau cooked in a ground in palm leaves that you say was interesting? There is not really pigs in Hawaii is there? Pigs live in barnyards at farms.

And besides you know about me being 42 years old, it is right about that I have been the most popular and number 1 employee of "Future Horizons" for quite a while now and that I will surely stay on being the most popular and number 1 employee of "Future Horizons" for the rest of my life until the day that I die comes. Which means that I will really stay on as the most popular and number 1 employee of "Future Horizons" for a long time to come.

And as for us Teresa (meaning you and me) besides us really having a really real true and special friendship together, I have taken a liking to you and you having had taking a liking to me meaning we have taken a liking to each other after you very first became a "Future Horizons" staff member sometime back in the year 2001, we have been friends together for 11 years now. And next year in 2012 it will be our 12th year meaning our 12th time for us having had been friends together.

It is time for this letter to be written to you goodbye. So goodbye friend.

Sincerely,
Mike P. Ferman

Why Mike Gave Up on Movies

Dear Teresa Corey,
Hiya Teresa. It is written in this letter to tell you to have you know that first of all, this is not a regular normal ordinary letter. This is a letter written to tell you just information about why Mike P. Ferman (namely me) gave up movies. I hope that you will understand

and think that these reasons about what made me give up movies are good reasons. Besides that you wrote back to me to tell me that you want to know about why I gave up movies.

Well to start off, one reason about why I gave up movies was because I had gotten tired of (and still am tired of) sequels movies. Do you know what sequels is? Maybe you will not know until you find out from this letter. A sequel is another movie that continues to the first movie. And sometimes there can be a 3rd sequel movie that continues to the 2nd movie. And sometimes there can be a 4th sequel movie that continues to the 3rd sequel movie, while the same story of what movie. And so on and so on and so on until sequels movies quits sometime when then there is not more movies of something like sequels.

That makes it then be almost too many movies. So then I thought that if I tried out and watched and liked a lot of sequels movies, I would then have too many movies of that kind to like and watch too many times.

So some sequels movies I have seen and some sequels movies I have not seen. Another reason why I gave up movies was because I had gotten tired of (and still am tired of) remake movies. Do you know what remake movies are? Maybe you would not know until you find out from this letter. Remake movies are where there is a movie and whatever the movie is called what? And then after a real real long time, another movie with the same story and the same name comes out. And then that other movie is a remake movie to the original one. With the same story and the same what name of the remake movie with different certain specific specific certain stars of people who were not in the original movie.

A 3rd reason about why I gave up movies was because I had gotten tired of (and still am tired of) comedy movies. Everyone knows what comedy is. Even you do too. Comedy is something like movies where there is funny moments parts that make people laugh. I hate it when most movies are mostly comedy movies because that makes that then seem like as if there is very much of other kinds of movies like drama movies.

Drama is something like movies where there is serious moments parts that do not make people laugh. And horror movies, besides that, horror in something like movies where there is scare moments parts that make people frightened. And suspense movies can be very much like drama movies. Besides that, suspense in something like movies where there is suspenseful moments parts that do not make people laugh. (At least I think that part written in this letter about suspense movies is right...I guess). And sometimes, some movies like dramas and musicals and action and adventure and science fiction and fantasy and children's movies have comedy (meaning funny moments parts) in them.

So some comedy movies I have seen and some comedy movies I have not seen. I have never seen a horror movie before in my life. Horror movies are too scary for me to try out. And they may be too scary for you to try out too (meaning you and me would never really try them out at all). And if you think that I have never tried out drama and suspense. You just don't know the names of certain specific drama and suspense movies that I have tried out.

A 4th reason about why I gave up was because I had gotten tired of (and still am tired of) children's movies. Some of them that are rated G. I feel tired of them because they are for children and since and since I am a teenaged man and not a little kid anymore, I do not look like a person who would have an interest in trying out children's G-rated movies anymore.

I have a few kinds of children's movies (some of them rated G) that I am always tired of. Like Walt Disney movies, cartoon movies, live action and live animation combined together and computer claymation movies. So some children's movies (some of them rated G) I have seen and some of them I have not seen.

A 5th reason about why I gave up movies was because I had gotten tired of (and still am tired of) rated PG-13 movies. I was tired of them being almost like rated R movies because of adult situation parts and language (meaning curse words) and violence. So some PG-13 movies I have seen and some PG-13 movies I have not seen.

A 6th reason about why I gave up movies was because I had gotten tired of (and still am tired of) rated R movies. I was tired of that kind of rated movies the most of all because of adult situation parts and language (meaning curse words) and violence and nudity. I hate it when most movies are mostly PG-13 movies and R movies because that makes that then seem like as if there is not very much of other kinds of rated movies like rated PG movies.

A 7th reason about why I gave up movies was because I had gotten tired of (and still am tired of) people of certain specific ones who carry around guns. Like police officers and secret agents and westerners.

An 8th reason about why I gave up movies was because I had gotten tired of (and still am tired of) people who get mad and upset and impatient and violent and say bad language words (meaning curse words) and have arguments. I do not like being like some people who get mad and upset and impatient and violent and say bad language words (meaning curse words) and have arguments. I hope you do not either. I think of myself as a gentle person. And I think of you as a gentle person too.

A 9th reason about why I gave up movies was because I had gotten tired of (and still am tired of) long movies meaning movies (of some) that run for several and several minutes. For example 108 minutes or 109 minutes or 110 minutes or 111 minutes and so on and so on and so on.

So some long movies I have seen and some long movies I have not seen. And something else in addition to that that I forgot to write to you about which is, some rated R movies I have seen and some rated R movies I have not seen.

A 10th reason about why I gave up movies was because I had gotten tired of (am still am tired of) movies (of some) about 2 people meaning couples. I hate it when most movies are mostly movies about 2 people meaning couples because that makes that then seem like as if there is not very much of other movies about 1 person or 3 people. So some movies about 2 people meaning couples I have seen and some movies about 2 people meaning couples I have seen.

And the 11th reason about why I gave up movies was because I am not going to try out some what kind of movies that can be ones that I know well that I cannot really enjoy. And a 12th reason about why I gave up movies was because I am not going to try out some what kind of movies that has some people of whoever in them that I really think is a waste of time.

There friend. That is my reasons of information written to you in this letter about what made me give up movies. If a few people from "Future Horizons" who are popular were to read this letter too, you might save this letter. So whatever you do, do not lose this letter. Okay?

Sincerely,
Mike P. Ferman

Chapter 10: Humor

Alex fell in love with playing with words, which resulted in some very bad puns. My friends all say his penchant for bad jokes is a genetic factor. (If you have a weak stomach, you may want to skip this part.) "Dad, let's not go to Long John Silver's—let's go to Short Jim Gold's!"

His brother, Justin, was looking for a job in the "ads," and Alex told him to try the "subtracts."

He was studying science and he came across the term, "prey on livestock." I was concerned that he wouldn't understand such a concept and asked if he knew what that meant. With a smile, he said that the wolves "prayed" over the animal before they ate it.

Alex went out to dinner with my friend, Polly McGlew, and her husband David. They were kind enough to take him to a very nice German restaurant. When the entrees arrived, he asked what the funny red stuff was on his plate. Polly patiently explained that it was "Rotkohl," a popular dish in Germany. She went one step further and said, "'Rot' is German for red, and 'kohl' means cabbage." Minutes later, David asked what route Polly took to the restaurant, as they had come in different cars. She replied, "I came up Cole Street."

Grinning, and without missing a beat, Alex said, "You mean Cabbage Street!"

When my son Xander was 5 years old, he made and ate a big piece of toast with jelly. As he joyfully ate it, some of it actually got into his mouth, but most of it went everywhere else.

"Xander, what is this all over your face?" I demanded.

"Cheeks!" he answered, to a question that to him probably seemed silly.

Carla Humbert, California

I was driving my sons Lance and Troy to school one morning and stopped at a red light. I quickly chatted with a friend who sells papers on the street corner. He put a paper in the car for me, and we drove away.

"Mom, you didn't pay. Did he give you that for free?" asked Troy.

"Yes, I have friends in high places, Troy." I joked.

Lance piped up, "You mean like in Canada and Alaska?"

Diane Murrell, Texas

My son Adam has a very healthy appetite but is still thin. One day, after a particularly robust meal, I told him he ate like he had a hollow leg. He agreed.

Later than night, as he prepared for his bath, I noticed his tummy sticking out because of his posture. I asked him if his tummy was full from eating.

He said, "No, but my leg is sure packed!"

Denise Komraus, Pennsylvania

One of our favorite people is Jerry Newport. A person with Asperger's syndrome himself, Jerry is the founder of a group called AGUA (Adults Gathering, United and Autistic), which brings together adults with Asperger's syndrome and high-functioning autism. Jerry is known for his kindness and his gentle, sensitive view of the world. However, he is equally recognized for his wit and sense of humor.

With tongue stuck firmly in cheek, Jerry came up with this list of ways you can tell you are a teenager or an adult with Asperger's. Enjoy!

You could have Asperger's syndrome if more than half of these apply to you:

1. You think Al Gore moves and talks normally.
2. As a child, rather than riding a bike, you turned it upside down and moved the pedals to watch the wheels turn.
3. Your think "Spin City" is a show about autism.
4. As a kid, you played with a hamster by putting him on a record turntable.

5. Your favorite movie of all time is "Groundhog Day."
6. You think Judge Judy should "chill" and just let everyone talk.
7. You believe that the action in World Wrestling Entertainment is real.
8. You see nothing funny in the "Who's on First" routine.
9. You could sing several stanzas of "Louie Louie" in church and not understand why it is not proper.
10. You would prefer a parrot to the speech therapist.
11. Your favorite kitchen utensil is the egg beater.
12. You think Bill Gates is "too cool."
13. You hate "Simon Says" and always lose.

Chapter 11:
Alex's E-mails

As a gift, and with some apprehension as to how it would be used, Alex was given a computer with e-mail capacity. To his mother's and my delight, he began using it and rapidly grew into the great communicator of the 21st century. Alex's "unique" perspective in verbal language made us smile and laugh when his words came through cyberspace. We did not change Alex's grammar, so you could get the "full flavor" of his words.

This first e-mail is to his sister (he really does know her first name!). Note that in this and virtually all other e-mails, Alex loves food and also assumes that the person he's e-mailing isn't very bright.

Dear Gilpin,

Actually Jennifer as I told you on the phone I am not going to camp after all. I do hope to see you this Friday. It was Saturday when I went to see the show called One. That same night we went to A Restaurant called Umberto's, it was A very nice Italian restaurant, and for dinner there I had the Shrimp Scampi it was very good. Another night while we were at Myrtle Beach we ate at another nice restaurant called the Parson's Table. I like it too for dinner there I had the Fillet Mignon it was A kind of steak which they take A piece of bacon and wrap it around the steak itself it was really good.

Love Alex

―――――

Dear Dad,

Thank you for these interesting thoughts. I really enjoyed them.

I really liked the one that said "A day without sunshine is like eh...night." I especially like that one. I sure had a fun time with you at Thanksgiving. I really liked the show called the Granbury Live. I actually liked the scene in that show where this girl tells Santa or whatever his name was that she wanted elves for Christmas and he thought she said she wanted Elvis for Christmas.

Once again I want to thank you for these interesting thoughts. I hope to be hearing from you soon. Take good care of yourself.

Goodbye.

Love Alex Gilpin

Dear Dad,

Thank you for the Top Country songs of the Day. I enjoyed reading them. As I told my Aunt Carole I do like Country music but I don't like to listen to it. I also want to thank you for the warning about when my M&M's Jukebox thing will come.

I hope we will have a good time in Baltimore this Christmas. I think you (and all of my aunts and uncles) are my number one reason I want to come to Baltimore. Because I wanted to see these people. I hope to be hearing from you soon. Take good care of yourself. Goodbye.

Love Alex Gilpin

———

Dear Jennifer Gilpin,

So Jennifer you went to see a movie called Amelie huh. You said that it was a good movie do you think I would like it? Well let me tell you while I was in Texas seeing my dad we went to two movies. One was called the Black Knight and the other one was the Harry Potter movie. Have you heard of the Harry Potter movie before? Well as I just told you the Harry Potter movie was the other movie I saw with my dad. I know that if you ask him, he'll tell you that that's the truth. I hope you have had great Thanksgiving. I want to hear all about it.

Did you have lots of Turkey, Ham, and/or Mashed Potato's and Gravy. Well I sure did. I had Turkey, Ham, Mashed Potato's and Gravy, and a Green Bean Casserole and it was all so good. I hope to hear from you soon. Take good care of yourself. Goodbye.

Love Alex Gilpin

Dear Aunt Carole,

I sure am glad your leg is healing. It would be bad news if it was getting worse. Aunt Carole when I told you that I had Chicken Fingers at the K&W Cafeteria I didn't mean that the chicken had fingers. I just meant that what I ate were like strips of fried chicken.

Tonight (12/3/01) Scott and I had another Social Skills thing with TEACCH and we were in two different groups (Yes Scott was in one group and I was in another one).

Guess what, when I went bowling with my group on one of my turns I got a strike (You know it's what you get when you knock down all the pins in one roll of your bowling ball).

Love Alex Gilpin

———

Dear Ms Colleen Gilpin,

That's great that you are going to California to visit my sister Jennifer and then to Hawaii. Now Ms Colleen Gilpin I want to hear about your trip when you come back home okay. My roommate Scott and A friend of ours named Shelley And I went to see the Disney movie called the "Princess Diaries" and I thought it was funny. I liked the two parts where the actors were playing baseball and the batter hits the ball and the ball hits other people. If you don't understand why I would think that was funny you might want to see the movie.

I hope you have A great time in California and Hawaii. Again I want to hear about your trip. Take care now. Goodbye.

Love Alex Gilpin

Here is an interesting view Alex has of one of the outstanding autism programs in the world, TEACHH (Treatment and Education of Autistic and Related Communication Handicapped Children).

Dear Aunt Carole,
I am so glad that you liked the part of my last E-mail where I had told you that I told two of the stories from my dad's book Laughing and Loving with Autism to the people who were at the TEACCH dinner and sitting at my table. TEACCH is a program held by Dr Gary Mesibov and it has something to do with autism.
     Goodbye.
     Love Alex Gilpin

———

Dear Jennifer Gilpin,
Yes we will be seeing each other at Jeffs wedding. It does sound like you had a lot of fun at Melanie's birthday party playing "Planet Hollywood" and playing "Outburst" and doing all the other things you had mentioned. Tell me when you were playing "Planet Hollywood" did you get any of the questions about movies or TV right? Also when you played "Outburst" did you guess any of the words on the word list? I sure hope you did.
     Let me tell you on Sunday night Scott and his community partner Diedre (Pronounced DEE-dra) and I went out for dinner at a restaurant called Sal's Pizzaria Ristorante (The last word in the name is pronounced REE-stor-ON-tey). At this restaurant I ate the Fettucini Alfredo with Shrimp on top. It was so good. Then on Monday night I went with a small group of members from TE-ACCH and we all went to a cafeteria in the University Mall called

the K&W. There I ate the Country Style Steak with Mashed Potatoes and Gravy and Creamed Corn on the side. Take care now.
Goodbye.
Love Alex Gilpin

Dear Aunt Carole,
So Pumpkin Pie is your favorite huh. In that case you must really like that kind of pie. I am so excited that Don will be getting a job at the Dollar General Store. I would like to hear all about what he does at his new job. So if you wouldn't mind telling me all about it I would appreciate it. Tonight Scott, and a couple of friends named Todd and Cristina, ate at a restaurant called Bailey's Pub and Grill. Did you know that the word Pub means bar? Well it does. Anyway there at the restaurant we all shared some Quesadillas. (Pronounced CASE-a-DEE-a's) as an appetizer. For my dinner though I ate a Bacon Cheeseburger with some French Fries. It was so good I loved it. I hope to hear from you soon. Take care now. Goodbye.
Love Alex Gilpin

Dear Aunt Carole,
Yes I'd love to send you my mother's E-mail address. Now Aunt Carole if you have A bad memory on E-mail addresses and if you have A printer you should print this E-mail out. Anyway here it is, it's swclement@... There now you have it. Also in case you don't

have my dad's E-mail address here it is it's dashgilpin@... There now you have my dad's E-mail address.

Take care now. Goodbye for now.

Love Alex

P.S. In case you saw that in this E-mails subject I put Starla Clement instead of Starla Gilpin and your wondering why it's because she is now married to A man named Nat Clement and she now got the same last name as Nat.

—————

The following was in response to a note I'd sent to Alex, telling him that he did not have to respond to joke e-mails.

Dear Dad,

Dad, the reason I replied to the E-mails about jokes and other interesting things is because I wanted to thank the person who sent me that interesting E-mail. In other words I thought it would be kind of rude for me to just not say anything at all. I didn't want to do anything that makes the people sending me those E-mails feel like they're not being a good enough E-mail sender. I just wanted to do what I can to make them feel good. I hope you understand that. I am glad to hear that the conference went well and that they LOVED the story about the linguini. I hope to hear from you soon.

Take good care of yourself. Goodbye.

Love Alex Gilpin

Alex was invited to his cousin's wedding and wrote about it, especially the food, with a surprise reference to yours truly.

Dear Aunt Carole,
Let me tell you about Jeffs wedding. His wedding went great.

To add to this wedding update the wedding was held at The Congressional Club in Washington DC. We had a great time at his wedding. We ate Fried Chicken and Salmon for dinner at the reception. It was really good food. There also was dancing and music at the reception too. But most of all I liked being with my dad. So I was glad that he was there. I think he is the nicest dad to be around. But again we had a fun time at Jeffs wedding. I actually wish you could have been there at his wedding. I will be hearing from you soon. Take good care of yourself. Goodbye.

Love Alex Gilpin

━━━━━

This e-mail shows Alex's sense of humor. It also shows his disinterest in segues.

Dear Aunt Carole,
Aunt Carole I know you think that I am a funny guy but I can't help it because I have a disease called "Saying Funny Things-tism."

It is a disease that makes me a funny guy. Yes I also have made my mother laugh before. So your birthday is on January the 25th huh. I hope neither you nor Uncle Larry let the dogs out again or else one of you might have to sing that song WHO LET THE DOGS OUT WOOF WOOF WOOF I will be hearing from you soon.

Take good care of yourself. Goodbye.
Love,
Alex Gilpin

Dear Aunt Carole,

I think we should do everything we can to protect this country from having any future terrorist attacks once and for all. Yes that is right because I (just like every body else) like our country very much. So I think we should let everybody live as long as possible. Again I think we should prevent any future terrorist attacks like the one that recently happened at the "World Trade Center" and the Pentagon in Washington DC.

If it is possible I would like you to print this E-mail out and share it with all the people you love very much in our remembering of the day these terrorist attacks happened. Yes the people I want you to share this E-mail with includes people in your family. This will show them how much I care about our country. I hope you agree with what I think about our country. What I said about keeping this country is what I think should happen to it especially for the people we love. Remember United We Stand and God Bless America. Take care now. Goodbye.

Love Alex Gilpin

P.S. Even though I am only 22 I would appreciate it if you would take what I said about this country seriously.

———

A discerning reader will find that the North Carolina basketball team did not have a very good year.

Dear Aunt Carole,

Aunt Carole yes I thought it was very sad that our team the North Carolina Tarheels lost on Thursday night. My roommate Scott really likes sports but I don't (okay at least not the way Scott likes them). As I told my sister Jennifer one time I do like sports but I don't like to watch them or play them. Do you like sports? If so what is your favorite sport?

Let me tell you what Scott and I did today (Saturday 11/3/01). Today Scott and I went with Scott's community partner Diedre (Pronounced DEE-dra) to a carnival at the dorm where Diedre stayed when she went to college at UNC (The University of North Carolina) called the Fall Carnival. At this carnival they had lots of food and games. The food I ate at this carnival was pretty good I ate some cupcakes and pretzels and candy corn and chips. I played two of the games there. One was Bingo (you know that game where they call out these numbers and if you get 5 in a row you call out Bingo) if you get Bingo you get a prize. Well guess what I did get a prize playing Bingo. The prize I got was a pumpkin with candy in it.

The other game I played was one called the Cake Walk (No we did not walk on a cake that is just what they called the game). The way this game is played is you have to walk on these numbers in a circle while the music is playing. Then when the music stops you stand on the number nearest to where you are.

I hope you are having a great day. Take good care of yourself. Goodbye.
Love Alex Gilpin

———

Dear Aunt Carole,
I actually do like violent movies. I just don't like to watch them. Yes I have heard some new Rock and Roll songs like Enya singing "Only Time." At least I think that is what the name of the song is.

Unfortunately, I forgot how this song goes. I certainly liked it when these trick or treaters came to your door and they said TRICK or TREAT to you and you gave them their candy then asked them where is the trick. Well Aunt Carole I don't think they mean there is a trick. I think it is just a saying kids use. I think you ought to know that by now.

I did go to a Pizza party (yes I did have pizza two nights in a row) and to watch the Georgia Tech vs the North Carolina Tarheels game. Sadly our team (the North Carolina Tarheels) lost. I hope you are having a great day. Take good care of yourself. Goodbye.

Love Alex Gilpin

Dear Aunt Carole,

I am sorry I didn't sign my last E-mail "Love Alex" at the bottom. I accidentally pushed the send button. Anyway as I was saying I don't know what we will be doing this weekend. I don't even know when the next time Scott and I will go bowling will be. Also I would like to make a correction. The song by Styx is called "Come SAIL Away With Me" not Come Fly Away With Me like you said. For information on what Scott and I did on Monday night and Tuesday night please refer to the last E-mail I ended up not signing "Love Alex Gilpin" at the bottom.

Love Alex Gilpin

Dear Aunt Carole,
No I didn't enjoy those Peanut Butter Cups that you gave me I just liked eating them Plus the ones that my mom gave me I didn't like them either I just liked eating them. Except that the ones that my mom gave me are a little bit bigger but that didn't stop me from enjoying them. I enjoyed them as much as I enjoyed the Peanut Butter Cups you gave me. Plus my grandmother Mati gave me some cookies and things like that (It was sent to me a little bit late but that's okay).

I miss you very much and hope to hear from you soon. Take good care of yourself. Goodbye.

Love Alex Gilpin

Dear Jennifer Gilpin,
Thank you for wishing me a Happy Valentine's Day. I want to wish you a Happy Valentine's day too. I hope you had a great Valentine's Day. I sure did. I didn't do anything special though. Did you get any Valentine's Day Candy? Well I sure got some Valentine's Day Candy from my mother. This Valentine's Day Candy is some Reese's Peanut Butter Cups with little Hearts on top and they were really good.

Just the other night I got an E-mail from my Aunt Carole telling me that she and Uncle Larry are going on a trip to Grand Field, Oklahoma and that while they are on this trip they are going to go to a drug store. You might never believe this but guess what the name of this drug store is (Hint think of my last name). If you said it is called the Gilpin's Drug Store you guessed it. That's right it is called the Gilpin's Drug Store. What do you think of that a Drug

Store with my last name? Wouldn't you be shocked if there was a place with the same as name as your name? Think about it. I again hope you had a nice Valentine's Day. Take good care of yourself.

Goodbye.

Love Alex Gilpin

—————

Dear Jennifer Gilpin,

I am sorry you didn't get any Valentine's Day candy. Maybe Valentine's Day isn't popular in the area where you live. Jennifer I would like to make a correction the name of the DRUG STORE that Aunt Carole is going to is the Gilpin's Drug Store it's not the name of the town like you said (At least I think that's what my Aunt Carole told me). I didn't share any of my Valentine's Day Reese's Peanut Butter cups although my roommate Scott did get some Reese's Cups too. He thought they were really good. Yes I really love my grandmother Mati very much and I thought that was very nice for her to think of me. I miss you very much and hope to hear from you soon. Take good care of yourself.

Goodbye.

Love Alex Gilpin

—————

Dear Jennifer Gilpin,

Yes, I did like the sweat shirt or whatever it was you gave me. Thank you for this shirt? By the way, did you get my email about what I did in Seattle, Washington, and in Baltimore, Maryland? If so, what did you think of it?

Let me tell you what Scott and I did today. Today, Scott and I went with a friend of ours named Todd to a basketball game. It was the North Carolina Tar Heels playing against the Wake Forest Demon Deacons. The final score was 84-62 and sadly our team (The North Carolina Tar Heels) lost. Scott and I sure would have been a lot happier if our team won. Although I heard that the Wake Forest Demon Deacons has a good basketball team. So I kind of thought we might lose. Again though, we weren't happy when we knew that our team (The North Carolina Tar Heels) lost. I hope to be hearing from you soon. Take good care of yourself. Goodbye.

Love Alex Gilpin

Dear Dad,

Dad I have two things to tell you. First of all I want to thank you for forwarding that E-mail called Hmmrn???? More food for thought! to me. I really liked it. I hope you will send more E-mails like this one because I like it a lot. Secondly I just want to remind you that my birthday is coming up. In fact it is this coming Wednesday when my birthday will be. Take good care of yourself.

Goodbye.

Love Alex Gilpin

In a way, the following may be the best e-mail Alex sent. He loved coming to the Future Horizons conferences, meeting the people, and enjoying the other speakers (not to mention the good food).

I offered to bring him to our conference in Maine, casually mentioning that, for this conference, we did not have room for his roommate, Scott, whom we often invite.

At first read, I was disappointed because Alex would not be coming. Then I realized the implication of Alex making a sacrifice for a friend.

Dear Dad,

I am feeling fine. I would rather not go to the conference in Portland, Maine, because of the fact that Scott will not be able to speak at that conference. I would like to come but not without Scott. He would feel bad.

I hope you have a great day and to be hearing from you soon. Take good care of yourself. Goodbye.

Love Alex Gilpin

———

Dear Jennifer Gilpin,

So you went to Boise, San Francisco, Ontario for work at conferences huh? Well I would like to know if these conferences were on autism. If so did my dad speak at any of these conferences? And if so did he tell the people at these conferences any of the funny stories about me? If so which ones do you know he told? Also when you do think of the name of that italian restaurant you celebrated your birthday Please tell me the name of it. I hope to hear from you soon. Take good care of yourself.

Goodbye.

Love Alex Gilpin

Is this a "subtle" hint for more?

Dear Mom,

Thank you for that nice shirt from Wyoming that you gave me. It was so nice for you to think of me. I think that I will wear this shirt soon that is how much I like the shirt. I sure hope you can give me more presents like this one in the future. I really would like it if you would do that. Once again thank you for the shirt.

    Love Alex

Dear Ms Colleen,

Thank you for the Irish Bracelet Message. That was very nice for you to think of me. You must be thinking of me A lot because you have been sending me A lot of E-mails. That must mean that you really like me as A friend (which I hope you do). I really like you A lot it's more than the fact that you send me these E-mails it's the fact that you are A very nice person in general. Once again though thank you for the E-mail on the Irish Bracelet. Take good care of yourself. Goodbye for now.

    Your friend Alex

Here, Alex assumes that Jennifer visits people she doesn't know.

Dear Jennifer Gilpin,

I sure am glad that you had a good weekend other than the shots that you had at the doctor. I think those are okay although they have stung me a little bit when the doctor puts that needle or whatever it's called in my arm but when you have to get a shot you have to get one. I don't think that's an optional thing.

You said that you are going to a friend's house to watch the ice skaters at the Olympics. What's this friend's name? Do you know? I hope you have a good time at this friend's house tonight. Please tell me all about it when you reply to this E-mail. I miss you very much and hope to hear from you soon. Take good care of yourself.

Goodbye.

Love Alex Gilpin

Alex—the spelling perfectionist?

Dear Mom,

Just so you know on the E-mail where you were telling me about work you spelled dear wrong when wrote dear Alex. When you spelled dear you left out the A.

Love Alex

Alex, who made whom late?

Dear Aunt Carole,

Saturday Scott and I were supposed to go to this Softball tournament but we ended up not doing that because of all of these mistakes that Scott made (I mean things like waiting for me to get out of bed and taking a late shower and things like that).

Then on Monday night Scott and I went to our Social Skills group. This group is actually split up into two groups. Scott's group went out to dinner at a restaurant called Lucy's. My group stayed at the TEACCH office and played a board game called Pictionary. Our group was split into two different groups for this game and to play this game you have to watch someone draw something and you have to guess what that something is. If you get the correct answer your team gets 1 point. And whichever team has the most points at the end of the game wins. And guess what my team won. I thought that was a good night. I hope to hear from you soon. Take good care of yourself. Goodbye.

    Love Alex

Alex, no need to hope...

Dear Dad,
I just want to wish you A Happy Birthday. I hope you will do something on your birthday (meaning something like going out to dinner). I really love you. I hope that you love me too. Goodbye for now.

    Love Alex

Chapter 12:
Poignant

The first *Laughing and Loving with Autism* had a concluding chapter called "Poignant." Although not planned at the conception of the book, it was very popular, and we have more wonderful and touching stories to share with you. These stories are from parents, siblings, and individuals with autism.

These stories also unintentionally reveal as much about the courage and hope of the writer as they do about their subject.

So, for your pleasure, here are offerings that give another perspective and a sensitive side to autism.

Children with autism prefer things to be constant. Change is generally not fun. That point is made quite evident here.

In our family, a favored weekend activity for my husband, Jim, and our 7-year-old son, Tim, who has autism, is to go for hikes on the nature trails in the city parks. This is followed by a trip to McDonald's. Naturally, this trip involves a very specific park exit to a very specific McDonald's. One Saturday, Jim attempted to vary the routine by taking a different exit. Tim became upset and protested. Jim tried to calm Tim down by telling him that "Different is not wrong."

Tim replied, "But Dad, to me, it is."

Nora Rege, Oregon

My normally developing grandson, Jeff, and I had just been to see "Aladdin." As we drove home, I asked him what three wishes he'd ask of the genie if he had the magic lamp. With no hesitation at all, he said, "First, I'd ask him to take away my brother Andrew's autism, and then I'd ask him to take away my Grandmom's Alzheimer's."

He paused a while, so I asked, "And what about the third wish? Something for yourself?"

"No, I think that would be enough, Pop," he said.

This is from the 9-year-old brother of a 4-year-old with autism.

Bill Hale, Virginia

One time, after I had admonished Alex about something, he and I had this conversation that shows how a child with autism will zero in to try to understand emotion:

Alex: "Do you like me?"
Dad: "You mean love...of course I love you."
Alex: "No—I know you love me, but do you like me?"

In a discussion with me, my son Alex tried to explain his challenge with autism (without realizing he was doing so):

Alex: "My brain doesn't work so good."
Me: "Now, or all the time?"
Alex: "All the time."
Me: "Mine doesn't, either."
Alex: "How doesn't yours?"
Me: "Remembering names. Why doesn't yours?"
Alex: "I don't know—I just can't make it think sometimes."

Starla Clement, North Carolina

———

This conversation with me shows the literal and, in a sense, realistic, way Alex treats emotions. His mother and I, who are divorced, discussed the possibility of Alex moving in with me. We were concerned about how he would react to that idea, so I suggested it to him innocently and was shocked by the response.

Me: "Alex, do you want to live with me?"
Alex: "Yes, I would...if my mother dies."
Me: "I, uh, well, um, uh—how would that make you feel? Would you miss your mother if she died?"
Alex: "Occasionally."

I'm a single parent of a boy with autism, Travas. He and I live in a rural area and have no access to other parents to share stories about the trials and heartaches autism brings. I can't rely on the public school system to address his needs nearly as well as I can at home.

Travas is low functioning and has a short attention span. He's 75% toilet trained and nonverbal. I sign to him with my hands all the time, but I've gotten no responses from him yet. We shower together daily and do hand-on-hand soaping and hair washing. We're presently working on how to use toilet paper.

Travas and I live in a large home in southern Utah on a 3-acre ranch. We have horses, ATVs, sailboats, a lake 10 minutes away, and much more. Sure, I enjoy these things, but most of this is for Travas and his recreational needs. We have only each other under this roof. It can be lonely, yet so fulfilling.

I'm not a wealthy man, but any and all extra money I receive goes into an account to better Travas and the world immediately surrounding around him. Travas enjoys his trampoline and swing set, and, with luck, maybe he'll enjoy a swimming pool in a few years! He loves water.

P.S. Donny Osmond is a neighbor, and he enjoys singing to Travas almost as much as Travas loves hearing him. Mr Osmond has a unique interest in Travas and often visits him. Travas has a unique interest in music.

Tony and Travas Tullius, Utah

Many school districts actively practice inclusion, making every reasonable effort to expose handicapped and/or special children to normally developing children, and vice versa. However, other school districts do not. In the following passage, Nancy speaks about the exclusion of these students in an eloquent and unique way.

One very snowy weekend at Deer Creek State Lodge changed the lives of three young boys forever—not to mention the lives of the adults who were privileged to be a part of that magical weekend.

The families came together in the most natural of ways. "Eric, this is my son, Gabe. Gabe, this is Eric. How old are you? Do you like swimming? Gabe is ten, and he swims like a fish. Would you like to join him after dinner?"

Eric seemed very timid about the water, especially the deep end of the pool. Every time Gabe got close, Eric felt compelled to inform me. I let him know that Gabe was a very good swimmer and actually preferred deeper water. Eric seemed surprised by that and took to keeping a closer eye on Gabe, not out of concern, but out of wonderment.

It was Saturday afternoon that I learned of Eric's near-drowning incident just the year before. No wonder he was so cautious and concerned about Gabe. As I watched the two engage in parallel play, a pattern emerged. Gabe swam up and played a brief game of catch. Eric followed Gabe to the deep end and swam from rope to ladder.

By dinnertime on the second day, the boys were best friends. They sat together at the table with smiling faces. Later, they shared special toys and it was evident they were creating a bond that only young boys can make.

Because of the bad weather, a third boy, Brian, did not arrive until just before dinnertime on Saturday night. All through the meal, Brian couldn't take his eyes off the two boys his age at the other table. Everyone was busy, so hasty introductions were made. "Brian, this is Eric and Gabe. Gabe, Eric, this is Brian."

By breakfast on Sunday, Brian was visibly straining to spend time with the other boys. He told his mom that he liked the way Gabe dressed. Finally, the three met up and spent a snowy morning sharing toys and food and fun.

This story is only remarkable if you know that Gabe is a child with autism and does very little communicating verbally. Eric has epilepsy and was afraid of the water. I'm not totally sure about Brian. He had "11-year-old-ism," which means he didn't really care about autism and epilepsy. He liked the way Gabe was dressed and thought Eric was a great guy.

When it was time to leave, Eric announced how Gabe had taught him how to swim. Gabe looked both Brian and Eric in the eyes and smiled a lot, and Brian was happy to have made some new friends.

I can't get past the pain of why this thing called "friendship" can't happen every day for Gabe. After all, it really didn't seem like hocus-pocus. It was just three boys being themselves, being "cool," being 11, being afraid. Since every child has a God-given right to just "be friends," why can't that happen every day? In school, it happens for millions of children all the time. Unless, of course, you are given a label and have to go to special classrooms with other special kids, with special teachers who know special things. As a result, this special education may not include much exposure to regular kids who don't really care about labels or disabilities but are very much interested in just being a kid.

My pain is not just for my son, but it's also for all the Erics and Brians who will never know guys like Gabe. Without exposure to each other, they won't be able to learn from his abilities or his "coolness" or make friends with him just because they want to and can.

Nancy Ray, Ohio

You are my little special child,
My funny valentine,
An accident of Providence?
Or are you by design?

It matters not the answer,
For you are here with me.
That you're not like the other kids
Is mighty plain to see.

But you are a worthy person
Who has come a long, long way.
Helping you has helped me grow
To where I am today.

There's something I must tell you,
Though the words are nothing new.
They've been sung so many times,
I say them now to you.

Is your figure less than Greek?
Is your mouth a little weak?
When you open it to speak
Are you smart?

Though other folks may think you odd,
You're my favorite work of art.
My funny little valentine,
You've slipped into my heart.

Claudreen Jackson, Michigan

Our son Pete has brought us so much laughter and joy. His good humor and love of life lighten up our days. A quotation from G. K. Chesterton epitomizes his beliefs: "An adventure is an inconvenience rightly viewed." Rather than being annoyed when it rains, he views it as being an adventure. For him, falling down when skiing is almost as fun as not falling down. Since Pete has come into our lives, I have changed my attitude toward life entirely. Nothing "stresses" me anymore. I make a stupid mistake, and I laugh. A broken egg on the floor is funnier than an intact egg. Every day with him brings laughter into our lives. Certainly, throughout the years I have been frustrated, desperate, angry, hopeless, and ready to give up, but after 49 years, the sum total of good times far outweighs all the bad.

Elizabeth Hirsch, New Mexico

When our son with autism was in his last year of public school, there was an aide in his classroom whom Mike could really relate to. Mr Craig was not much older than Mike was, and Mike followed him around and imitated his every move—placing his hands on his hips, scratching his head, and shooting the basketball. Whatever Mr Craig did, Mike did too. Mr Craig taught him the "high-five" handshake, and the two greeted each other with it every day.

The school year ended, and Mike no longer saw his friend. A year passed, and then one day as Mike and I were leaving the shopping center, from across the parking lot someone shouted, "MIKE!" Mike looked up and saw Mr Craig. The two of them raced toward each other and gave each other the "high-five" with big smiles. What a thrill it was to see the joy on Mike's face upon seeing his friend again by surprise.

Monica Moran, Texas

When he was just a little fellow, Scott learned very quickly to dress himself and brush his teeth. But he couldn't tie his shoes. Scott was slow in talking and was 7 or 8 years old before that came together. Now, at 27, he has little difficulty in expressing himself. He keeps himself well groomed and gets an "A" in hygiene. His athletic ability, especially when it comes to bowling, is somewhere between "the norm" and "above the norm." He loves all sports and finds ways to play them alone. But, he still hasn't been able to tie his shoes.

He's kind, caring, and tries so hard to find his place in society.

Scott's growing ambition now includes working year round (at the Sheltered Workshop), which is one GIANT step for this young man.

Scott operates our home computer and plays computer games, but he mostly practices his typing lessons with 100% accuracy. Still, he has not been able to tie his shoes.

Last week, a friend of mine showed me a simple, double-knot way to tie a shoe. I, in turn, showed Scott this simple method—and he has been tying his shoes ever since!

What's next, Scott? It's up to you. You have climbed such a steep mountain, with just a short distance left to the "Summit of Success." I acknowledge you for making your slow and deliberate climb in the right direction.

Go get 'em.

Jean Butler, Maine

Some people with autism have high-level splinter skills but still have problems interacting with people in society. The following contribution comes from such an individual. Jerry has a math degree but has not benefited financially from that accomplishment. His words may give you insight into a "savant" type of person, with a different view of life but a very poignant closing.

I enjoy sharing my autism history with groups, but introductions are the hardest. Talking about my birthplace is confusing. It has always seemed that I was born on another planet and snuck into Little Falls, New York, under a full moon, on August 19, 1948—a Thursday.

I must come from the planet Newportia, by way of New York. Welcome to my world! Here, everything happens on time. People always mean what they say. You never have to do more than one thing at once. If you don't do it right at first, just try again. That is as Newportian as potato-chip pie.

Everything necessary has been made and lasts forever. Since TV sets, radios, and cars have only one channel, station, or gear, this makes sense. The streets are paved with pizza. Edible clothes and furniture are the rage.

Newportia has no crime. Giant parrots patrol my planet. They eat all criminal invaders. Our only work is feeding the parrots. Newportians bring bowls of fruit and popcorn to their beautiful friends. The popcorn comes from movie theaters. The theaters feature two shows: "Dumbo" and "Pinocchio."

The Newportia I fancy I come from usually seems like a post-card kind of life to me. But, I can get along on this earth. Remember this: The reality and behaviors of all people with autism are just as sensible to them as your life is to you. To ensure the fullest life possible for you and your children, you must accept them as human beings in every way.

Jerry Newport, Michigan

———

I try to remind myself of all the things that Sam can do, and enjoys doing, instead of dwelling on all the "shortcomings." Of course, this is what I should do with all people. I try to stay hopeful about the future...about the support that will be available in school, at home, and in the community that will enable Sam to become independent and productive. I also try to stay hopeful about the natural progress that Sam is going to continue to make, even though it happens at a slow, unpredictable pace. I try to stay hopeful about my relationship with Sam...in that even though he tests me a great deal and can be aggressive toward me sometimes, I will find better ways to interact with him so we can progress together as he matures.

Sam is an integral part of the Russell family experience. We are who we are because he is a part of us. He is who he is because of the family he is a part of. I value this more than I can possibly communicate. Would I give away Sam's autism? Gladly! Would I give away the compassion and social awareness he has brought to my heart and the hearts of my daughter, husband, and extended family and friends? Never! God has really used Sam to shape our lives, and I marvel at the strength of character, wisdom, and acceptance I see in my daughter—traits I never had at her young age and will never have in the natural, easy manner she does.

Anne Russell, Texas

You just found out your child has autism?

It's not all that bad, folks!

Sure, having a child with autism in the family does cause some problems, and parents must change a lot of their preconceived notions about childrearing. But, that's not necessarily bad. For instance, our son, Buz, has needed many years of speech therapy, special education, summer camps, and 14 months of hospitalization. However, I feel that this "challenge" has given us an advantage other parents don't have. These teachers, therapists, and doctors have been the most caring, nurturing people we've ever known. With generations of families so widely scattered these days, how many parents have the benefit of such a tightly knit support system?

Buz has helped us get to know the people in the neighborhood, and indeed the entire city. He has always been innocently curious. Buz will go up to strangers and ask all about the supermarkets in their areas and the pipe organs in their churches. They quickly realize that they are dealing with a very lovable—though unusual—person.

Once people get to know Buz, they like him very much and feel somewhat protective of him. It's not uncommon for me to meet people for the first time who live many miles from my home, who break out in a smile and say, "Oh, you're Buzzy's mother!" He just seems to bring out the best in people. He has made all of our lives better and more fulfilling.

Sometimes I feel sorry for families with only "regular" kids. Their lives must be so boring!

Sandy Grabman, Oklahoma

The first step in my plan to get back into shape was to join an aerobics class. This was a new venture for me, having never before joined an organized exercise class. All of my previous efforts had been personal and individual.

The first class was a personal disaster. Not only was I out of breath as I tried to keep up with the other participants, who were in better shape and were mostly younger than me, but I was also having trouble following the instructions quickly.

My son James, who has autism, was there as I explained to my normally developing daughter, Jennifer, how I had embarrassed the family name that day. I laughed as I explained how, when the rest of the class was up, I was down. When they were moving forward, I was moving backward and was always, always one beat off.

Jennifer was delighting in my story. We weren't sure James was even listening. He obviously was, however, because he surprised us both by speaking up and saying, "Yeah, Mom, it was just like autism, huh?"

At the time, I was too amazed at his perception to respond. But, yes, James, I suppose what happened to me was very much like how you experience the world.

Nancy Deaves, Ontario, Canada

My son Jeremy's teacher is very good at saving special papers for me that he does in class. Since he generally throws all his schoolwork and notes from the teacher away before he gets home, I really appreciate it when she manages to save one. One paper I will treasure forever is a writing assignment he had to do about someone important to him. It was particularly significant because I don't often hear these thoughts:

"My mother is a teacher at Miss Jewell Elementary *[sic]*. My mother is also a great mother. She loves me much. I like her even if she gets mad at me. I love her."

Bonita Gallen, Texas

Alex stayed with his mother during the summers and enjoyed it very much. One summer, she arranged for him to take voice lessons. He seemed pretty happy about it, as he loved almost any contact with music. She came to pick him up after a lesson and arrived a little early. Not wanting to embarrass him, she waited in the hall.

From there she could hear him, but he couldn't see her. Tears ran down her face as she stood outside the door, listening. It wasn't because of the quality of his singing; rather, it was the song he sang. Alex, a child for whom there had been so many gloomy predictions, was singing, "You'll Never Walk Alone."

The following was written by a 9-year-old boy about his feelings for his brother.

My Brother David

I don't think people should make fun of handicapped people because they are different, in different ways. I don't think people with autism are mean or bad, they are just different from us. They were born that way.

My brother is handicapped. I don't like it because my brother can't play football with me—he does not understand. I told him to make a touchdown, but he just stood there. I had to show him what to do. If I tell my brother to do something, he will yell at me, and I get scared. One time, when we were playing with toys, my friend was over and we went upstairs. David was playing "Jurassic Park." I asked David if he would play with me and my friend. He got mad and threw toys at us.

My brother goes to a special class with other handicapped kids. I feel sorry that he has autism, but I'm still lucky to have a brother. I don't like it when he imitates me, but that's how he learns things from me. I would be alone if he were not here, and I wouldn't have anyone to play with very often.

I know he is not the way other people are used to, but I love him. Even if he is not like everybody else.

Dale Limbrock, Michigan

―――――

When you have a handicapped child, there are a lot of times people make cruel comments or say things that they think will help but are inappropriate.

There are, however, those occasions when someone says something that does help and will stay with you for a lifetime. One such comment came from my father, the day we told him that his grandson was handicapped.

That day, as my husband and I sat with my parents at their kitchen table, I was very nervous. I wasn't sure how they would take the news. We said we had something important to tell them about David. When we told them he had autism and was mentally handicapped, I started to cry. I looked at my mother and could see the tears beginning to form in her eyes. My father looked up at us and said firmly, "He's still our grandson—he's still our David."

In that moment, I knew he was right. Nothing had really changed. He was still David. He was still the same little boy we loved so much. David is fortunate to have grandparents who love him for who he is, without qualifications.

Brenda Limbrock, Michigan

My son, Micah, has autism. Although he is verbal, his speech is limited. He has come a long way in the past few years, but there was a time when I wondered if Micah would ever use meaningful language to communicate. I wanted so much for him to tell me his favorite color, what was behind his fascination with stop signs, or what he wanted for Christmas. Anything spontaneous would have been appreciated. Most of all, I wanted to hear him say to his mama, "I love you."

One wonderful day, I rented the Walt Disney movie, "Beauty and the Beast." Micah loved it—especially the music. When the movie was over and the credits began to roll, I got up to leave the room. Micah stopped me and took hold of my hands. At first, I thought he was afraid I was going to turn off the tape before the credits were finished (an unforgiveable crime to Micah's way of thinking).

However, I was surprised when Micah looked up at me and, in his own language, asked me to dance. As the credits rolled and the theme played, my son laid his head against me and slowly began to sway. When the song was over, he stopped "dancing," looked me straight in the eye and said, "I love you, Mama." The words were soft and a bit slurred, but they were unmistakably genuine.

It's been 2 years since Micah first spoke his words of love. I am still moved every time I recall his gift to me. As he continues to grow and learn, I find myself taken with the way Micah makes up with me after we have had some kind of disagreement. When all is said and done, Micah brings the situation to a close by saying, "I still love you, Mama."

Beverly Phillips, South Dakota

Empty Noises

Looking at you
looking somewhere else in McDonald's.
Happy meals and fries
don't fill the empty silence
amid the chaos.
The constant chatter
of other 3- and 4-year-olds
surrounds you and me.
In the car
on the way home
I ask
"Was your cheeseburger good?"
In the rear view,
I notice a mother and son
(about the same age as you and me)

talking back and forth in the front seat.
Their conversation seems to never end
as we wait for the light to turn green
in our silence.

Connie Post, California

———

In my profession as an autism consultant, I met a delightful young lady who has an older brother with autism. My conversations with her consisted of the normal range of ups and downs but also evidenced her strength, as she said that anyone who could not accept her brother wasn't a friend anyway. However, she helped me realize that a sibling doesn't merely deal with what is there but also with what she is missing, particularly in an older brother. The confidant, protector, and mentor roles that a younger sister hopes to find in an older brother simply can't be realized. Still, she spoke of hope and love. Her poem that follows was one I found very touching.

Cindy Waddell, Oregon

Brother

What goes on behind your eyes
in your mind?
I want to know,
are you real?
Sometimes, I'll see a glimmer
and maybe I'll hope
but I get afraid
and crawl back into my shell...just like you.
There are things I want to say to you
and do for you
because you're my brother.
Aren't you?
You have your walls
and I have mine.
Do I try hard enough to break your walls down?
How hard should I try?
Could you even tell me
or do I have to be strong by myself?
One day, your walls will come down
your shell will break open,
and I'll find a way to say to you
Hello...I am your sister...you are my brother
and I've always loved you.

Donnie

Whenever Alex's sister went out for a drive, I always said, "Turn on your lights and lock the doors."

One day, Alex asked, "Why do you always say that, Dad?"

I was a bit taken aback, but, after consideration, I offered what I thought was an answer that would satisfy his question. I said, "It is really my way of saying, I love and care for you."

He looked pensive as he played with his fingers, as he always did when he concentrated. Then he looked up and said, "Why don't you just tell her that you love her and care for her?"

The logic of that comment so overcame me that I had no reply.

Three weeks later, I threw on my jacket and adjusted my tie as I rushed out of the house, since I was late for an appointment as usual.

Alex, aiming his voice at me but looking at the floor, said, "Dad, turn on your lights and lock the doors."

About the Author

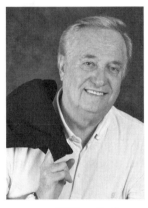

Wayne Gilpin founded the Future Horizons publishing company in 1996 to focus on generating resources about autism. Before that, he published car repair guides and law books. But, his son Alex's diagnosis of autism rerouted his career path.

Wayne joined the Autism Society of America (ASA) in 1987 and was voted president in 1988. He guided the ASA through a very difficult financial period and managed to erase all debt in less than a year. On a personal level, he collected as much information on autism as he could, but he was concerned by the fact that all of the resources available were negative and offered little hope for him or his son's future.

However, experiences with Alex told a different story. His son was a gentle, honest, and intelligent person, and Wayne was confident that Alex would overcome his obstacles and defy the odds. To bring a little light into the autism community, he compiled and published a little book called Laughing and Loving with Autism, which contained humorous and touching stories from parents of children with autism. It was the first book to really capture the positive aspects of kids like Alex, and it gave other parents hope.

At first, Wayne expected that the market for this book would be confined to presents for his friends and family, or perhaps a few friends might buy a copy. However, he quickly found that parents he met had similar negative feelings about the current offerings and wanted copies of the book for themselves. Additionally, there were educators who wanted to better understand the viewpoints of those with autism and were interested in this new perspective.

And so, an important new chapter of Wayne's life began to fold. As a publisher already, he knew that a new book, in a new field, was not likely to receive much recognition. He had 500 copies printed and assumed it would take at least a year to have them purchased or given away. Instead, all 500 sold in 3 days.

Because his name was so well known in the autism world through his work with the ASA, others began to come to Wayne with their books. The reception to these titles and the more than 140 to follow over the next 14 years was beyond his wildest expectations. To supplement the books, he began offering conferences that featured the authors.

Now, the titles offered by Future Horizons are distributed in 20 languages in more than 50 countries. From an idea of helping parents see the benefits and positives of having a child with autism has evolved a company, which serves a need that no one knew existed 20 years ago. Future Horizons is not only recognized as a leader in the field of autism, but it is also respected as an outstanding small publishing company—among the best in the world.

Future Horizons has become the largest publisher of autism materials in the world today because of love. Not a love of profit or glory—but the love of a son.